Landing on My Feet

Landing on My Feet
A Diary of Dreams

❀

Kerri Strug with John P. Lopez

Andrews McMeel
Publishing

Kansas City

www.andrewsmcmeel.com

Library of Congress Cataloging-in-Publication Data

Strug, Kerri, 1977-
    Landing on my feet : a diary of dreams / Kerri Strug with John P.
Lopez.
        p. cm.
    ISBN 0-8362-3708-0
    1. Strug, Kerri, 1977- . 2. Gymnasts—United States—Biography.
3. Women gymnasts—United States—Biography. 4. Olympic Games
(26th : 1996 : Atlanta, Ga.) I. Lopez, John (John P.) II. Title.
GV460.2.S77A32   1997
796.44'092—dc21
[B]   97-18319
                                                                  CIP

Attention: Schools and Businesses
Andrews McMeel books are available at quantity discounts with bulk purchase for educational, business, or sales promotional use. For information, please write to: Special Sales Department, Andrews McMeel Publishing, 4520 Main Street, Kansas City, Missouri 64111.

For my family and coaches, and in memory of my friend and former teammate Hilary Grivich
—Kerri Strug

For Mom and Dad, who sacrificed so much. And for Jan, Jacob, BG, and Leah
—John Lopez

Contents

❀

Acknowledgments

❀

All my life, I have been fortunate and blessed to have so much support from friends and family. On the way to completing this project, that support was as strong as ever. There are so many people to thank. First, my family, and especially Mom and Dad. Then my coaches, teachers, physical therapists, physicians, and friends, who all have seen me through so much. John Lopez and I want to express our deep appreciation to the following: USA Gymnastics, and especially Kathy Kelly, for her constant support, and Luan Peszek, for providing so much statistical information and help; David Black, for doing so much to put this project together; the fine people at Andrews McMeel, and especially Chris Schillig, whose editing touch and talent are unsurpassed, and Jean Zevnik and JuJu Johnson; Gary Morris; the *Houston Chronicle*, and especially Dan Cunningham, Reid Laymance, and David Barron; and the Roys, Pryors, Smiths, Ossulburns, Gurneys, and Tony Richards, for their technical support and friendship.

And finally, an extraspecial thanks to my teammates. For everything.

Prologue

❀

More than a billion people watched me limp and wobble to the brink of my dream. With every step, I shook out my leg, trying to ignore the numbing pain that suddenly pierced my left ankle. As the Georgia Dome fell silent, I walked to the top of the vault runway, searching for hope in the words that bounced through my head.

"You can do it, Kerri."

I had heard my coach, Bela Karolyi, utter those words a million times. I spent many years telling myself those same words. I believed in Bela and I always believed I could achieve my greatest dream of becoming an Olympic champion.

But this was the most critical moment of a lifetime spent enduring challenges and setbacks. Of the billion people watching the Olympic team gymnastics finals on that hot, overcast Atlanta afternoon in 1996, few knew how often I had been pushed into the background, thrown into the shadows through a sudden twist of fate, an untimely heartbreak or an injury that threatened to end my career. Very few people knew why I kept going in spite of everything and faced only one choice on that unforgettable day in Atlanta. My only choice was to try the final vault of the competition. After fourteen years of putting up with so many difficulties and sacrifices, the pain and pressure of one moment were not going to stop me from giving my dream one more run. I wasn't trying to be a hero. I was trying to hit the routine of my life.

It's rare that an Olympic gymnastics competition hinges on a single moment, rarer still when a person's life does the same. But on that July 23 afternoon, the first Olympic team gold in U.S. gymnastics history hinged on the 77.3 feet that stood between me and the spot on which I would vault myself into the air and land who knows where. Olympic glory? Infamy? I only knew that one way or another, there would be closure for all the wounds left open after fourteen years of devoting everything to the sport I loved.

As I stood there at the takeoff point, waiting for the judges to flash the green light that would tell me I could begin my routine, I reached down, grabbed my foot, and twisted it in circles, trying to wring out the pain. All I could hear were crackling, snapping sounds. Moments earlier, the unthinkable happened, considering how strong I'd been for six months before the Games—I fell. On my favorite event and my favorite vault routine, the Yurchenko 1½, I landed short and sat down in front of 32,000 people at the Georgia Dome and a billion more watching on television.

My fall gave the Russians hope that they could steal away the gold medal in the final moments of the competition, as they had done so many times before. Earlier, my teammate Dominique Moceanu fell on both of her vaults, and our seemingly insurmountable lead suddenly looked fragile.

Our USA team had one chance to clinch the gold. I had one vault and one moment to score high enough to win, but there was so much pain in my ankle. When I fell on my first vault, I turned it badly and felt a severe pop. I knew something definitely was wrong, but I had only seconds to either try the final vault or walk off the podium and leave the gold medal up for grabs. For me, that decision had been made years before I made the walk to the top of the runway.

I stood there under the lights, staring at the vault 77.3 feet away, listening to the tense silence all around me. I said a quiet prayer and told myself, "You can do it, Kerri."

It was a day on which my life began a new journey. It was a day when I learned once and for all that no matter how much you try to prepare for every conceivable possibility in your life, there always are unexpected surprises. For me, some of those surprises were devastating. Some were wonderful. And one strange, unexpected moment in Atlanta proved that just when you believe your dreams have been shattered, everything can come together and you're vaulted into a world where dreams come true.

After all the years and all the experiences, that's why I carried my diary with me to Atlanta. I had managed to overcome so much. I had grown up so much. I wanted to share every moment with my diary. And that is exactly what I did, throughout the whirlwind of attention the 1996 "Magnificent Seven" team received. Throughout the training and preparation with my teammates—Shannon Miller, Dominique Dawes, Jaycie Phelps, Amy Chow, Dominique Moceanu, and Amanda Borden—I turned to my diary. After the compulsory competition, when we finished .127 of a point behind the Russian team going into the final day, I told my diary about how close we were to the gold.

Finally, when July 23 arrived and we were only hours away from possibly making U.S. gymnastics history, I opened my diary one more time before joining my teammates in the van that would take us to the team finals. I wrote out an assertion that I always made to myself when things were tough.

"Kerri, you can and you will have an outstanding performance. Show the world how hard you've worked."

It had been a tense few hours before we boarded the vans. We hardly spoke to each other at breakfast or around the fraternity house at Emory University, where we stayed during the Games. By the time we loaded into the van, you could see the pressure in all our faces. The ride was extremely quiet. In fact, the only person I remember speaking was Dominique Dawes, who asked if someone could go back to the house for the official USA athletic shoes she had forgotten to pack in her bag.

"I'm not going to be the only one on the awards stand who's not wearing shoes," Dominique said.

We all forced a little laugh. When we got to the Georgia Dome, there was so much energy everywhere. The crowd was unbelievable, even when we were behind a curtain stretching, waiting to warm up. Every once in a while a fan would shout, "Let's go, USA," or "Come on, Shannon," or "Stick it, Dominique!" We walked behind the bleachers where the media sat and could hear people speaking in every language you could imagine. The atmosphere was incredible. Tickets for team finals were going for $1,000 apiece outside. Even paying face value for their tickets, my parents spent a fortune on them.

A few of the girls tried to play cards as we waited to warm up, but most of us were too nervous. I wore my leotard pulled up to my waist and a big white T-shirt with the Olympic rings imprinted in gold on it. I got my ankles taped and then began stretching and running in place, feeling that familiar sting of newly wrapped tape cutting into my skin. I got my shins taped— they had been really sore since the Olympic Trials. I lay back, closed my eyes, and ran through every routine in my head. Move for move, I told myself a key word that would take me through every second of every routine. "Bars: Smooth, straight, stretch, catch, clean, long, tall, stretch, smooth, catch, tight, kick, straight, big tap, swing, stick."

There. The perfect bar routine. I visualized the same for every apparatus. I went through the rotations exactly as I hoped to do them that afternoon. Finally I got to the vault, my favorite event. Just a few months earlier, I had begun doing the Yurchenko 1½, which is graded internationally as a 10.0 vault. In other words, it is the toughest vault a gymnast can do. A lot of fans often wonder why some routines that look as if they were performed perfectly are actually scored lower than others that have a slight bobble. It's because the perfect routine probably started out with a 9.9 or 9.8 international scoring code, and the slightly flawed one began as a 10.0.

The tougher the vault, the tougher it is to pull off, the higher the starting grade and the more the judges respect you. The Yurchenko is the toughest possible, which meant that if I completed it cleanly I could score a 10.0. It also meant that I might be able to bobble a little bit and still earn a good score.

"Speed, mark, steady arms, stretch, good block, tight turn, stick." In my mind, I did a perfect Yurchenko. Finally it was time to get ready for the competition. We were in the final group to compete in the team finals, along with Russia, Romania, and Ukraine. We had been waiting all our lives for that moment and it was impossible not to worry about every detail. As I was warming up, I sneaked a look at the big video screen hanging overhead and saw the Chinese team finishing their competition on the vault. I noticed that some of them were sticking the same vault I was going to use, a Yurchenko 1½, but they were being scored with a bunch of 9.6s.

"Oh, no," I thought. "They're scoring the vault really low today."

The vault, I knew, would be the key to our gold-medal hopes and for my individual all-around hopes. A 9.6 would not be good enough.

Martha Karolyi, Bela's wife and another of my coaches, urged me to concentrate on what I was doing, and it refocused me on the warmup. Still, I looked up at the screen one more time during warmups and noticed that my friend Svetlana Boguinskaia of Belarus, who trained with me in Houston for a while, had fallen on her bar routine.

"Oh, no," I thought. Svetlana had worked so hard to make it back to the Games. She was twenty-three, which is considered old for elite gymnastics. She was competing in her third Olympics and was a legend among us.

"Kerri, Kerri, concentrate!" I heard Martha say again.

The rest of the warmup went really well and finally it was time to start. "Well, here it is," I told Dominique Moceanu.

"Let's hit everything," she said.

This is all a gymnast ever dreams about: Just hit everything. It's all I ever wanted, but for me, for a lot of reasons, it didn't always work out that way. I funneled everything in my life toward the routines and only the routines. Even when I did manage to hit, it seemed there was always someone else hitting just a little bit sharper, scoring a little bit higher, competing a little big tougher. Kim, then Shannon, then Dom.

There was always someone or something that made me open a new diary and write, wondering why I was always the one sitting in the back of the room crying.

Why didn't things ever work out the way I planned? Why did coaches doubt me? Why did I always compare myself with others? How could I love this sport so much and feel unfulfilled by it at the same time? Why did the worst injuries come at the worst of times? When was it going to be my turn to hit everything?

It's all I ever wanted. And all I ever planned.

1

"Dr. Strug, your little girl has the perfect body for this sport"

❀

I prepared the list probably two weeks before my eighth birthday, carefully outlined on a notepad and very neatly handwritten.

I've always been very big on lists and planning. That's how I am about everything in my life—I like to plan things down to the last detail. Whenever I pull out a notepad and pen, my family and friends start to laugh. "Oh, there goes Kerri with another one of her famous lists."

My house is littered with scraps of paper with neatly numbered lists of things to do on them. If someone asks if I want to go to the movies, I'll grab a newspaper and pen and start carefully going through the possibilities. I'll circle some movies and cross out others. For as long as I can remember, I have liked to be prepared for every conceivable possibility in my life.

For my eighth birthday, my mom said I could invite a few friends over for a party, so I began outlining the perfect day. As it turned out, my idea of a perfect day was drastically different from my friends' idea of a perfect day. And that was probably the first time I realized that I took gymnastics a bit more seriously than most people do.

The day's itinerary went like this: "Two o'clock, my friends arrive here. Two-fifteen, put on *Nadia*. Four o'clock, cake and presents. Four-thirty, play in the backyard, party ends."

Most people probably don't remember the movie *Nadia*. It certainly isn't a film classic, and if you asked for it at a video store today, the person behind the counter would probably give you a blank stare. But to me, that movie about Nadia Comaneci's life and her 1976 Olympic Games experience was worthy of an Academy Award. It was *Gone With the Wind*, *Casablanca*, and *Star Wars* all rolled into one. A timeless classic. My treasured copy of the movie is still stored at my parents' house.

As a child, I watched *Nadia* at least two or three hundred times, and by my eighth birthday I already knew every word by heart. I watched it in the mornings while I got dressed for school. I watched it once or twice after school or gymnastics practice. I watched it on weekends. I took it with me on vacations. Every word was etched in my mind, which was a blessing for my family because they could tell me to turn down the volume and I'd still watch the screen in rapture, quietly reciting every word to myself.

By my calculations it was going to be a great birthday party. As my mom and I prepared for everyone to arrive, I lined up chairs in front of the television in our family room and slid Nadia's story into the VCR. Outside, it was another sunny, warm day in Tucson. From the backyard of our house, which is located near Sabino Canyon in the Tucson Country Club area, Mount Lemmon looked beautiful as usual. I've always loved our house, a ranch-style one-story my parents bought when they moved from Houston before I was born.

I can't count the times I've been in a strange room in some strange house in a strange city or country, all alone, picturing myself walking through the front door of that house and straight into my parents' arms. It's the safest place I ever knew.

For my party, I invited about ten friends, most of them from my school, Armstrong Primary Academy, and a few from gymnastics class. As my friends began arriving I ushered everyone into the family room and started the movie. I had seen *Nadia* with my friends before, but this was going to be special. There we all were, on a beautiful Saturday afternoon with cake and games and toys all around, watching *Nadia* together.

Only ten minutes passed before the first few girls drifted off to play in the backyard. Eventually they all left to play on the swings or in my room or to run around the house. By the time the movie was over, one of my gymnastics friends, Tara Murray, and I were the only ones still sitting there. I'm pretty sure the reason Tara didn't get up and join the others was because, as they were leaving, I shot her a threatening look that said, "You'd better not move a muscle." Tara and I watched every moment of the movie. I was hurt and angry that my friends didn't understand my love for gymnastics. It was *my* party and there I was surrounded by a bunch of empty chairs.

I wish I could say that was the precise moment when I realized I would become an Olympian. I wish I could say I knew right then and there that I would dedicate my life to winning a gold medal no matter what it took. But that would be a lie. I wasn't that confident then.

What I did realize was that this sport completely captivated me. I liked playing outside, too. I liked parties, swing sets, riding my bike, eating cake and ice cream, reading magazines, playing with dolls, swimming, hide-and-seek, teddy bears, Barbie. Everything that little girls like, I liked, too.

But I knew I would gladly pass on all those things to devote more time to gymnastics. Even as an eight-year-old, I was impressed by the way Nadia moved and performed, the way

Mary Lou Retton competed, the way my sister Lisa practiced.

No matter how much my parents tried to interest me in something else, no matter how many parties and holidays I missed, no matter how devastated I was when my sister was injured or had to leave home because of gymnastics, I fell in love with the sport in 1984. I was obsessed with it. I ate, drank, and slept gymnastics.

I'd been involved in the sport for about four years by the time I was eight. I wasn't competing yet, but I had participated in a few exhibitions with my team from the Gymnastics Center. A few of Lisa's out-of-town coaches said I had talent and tried to persuade my parents to let me join their clubs, too. But my parents thought I was much too young to leave home. Still, I knew a lot of tricks already and loved the sport. Lisa is eight years older than I, and it all started when I began copying her gymnastics moves when I was about four. I drove with Mom to drop off Lisa at her gymnastics practices and just sat there, fascinated by all the things she and her teammates were learning. I stood along the sides of the gym, trying the same moves. Sometimes after her practice, Lisa would teach me a few moves. I was surprised at how easily I could do the acrobatics. Often after I got home from watching Lisa's practices, I frolicked around the front yard pretending to be a gymnast. Later, once I began going to my own practices, I spent time walking around the house making believe I was Nadia or Mary Lou.

If while we were eating dinner my father asked me to get him something from the refrigerator, I would hop out of my chair and do a balance beam routine along the lines of our tiled floor. Chin up, toes pointed, flipping and landing.

"Kerri, just get the butter," my father would say in exasperation.

Whenever my mom asked me to clean up my room or do some other chore, I usually did a few handsprings or cartwheels along the way. Every curb on every street was a balance beam. Every swing set was an uneven bar. My dad used to tell me that I was the least expensive child he had: The only present I ever wanted was a leotard, and I never wore out my shoes because I was always walking on my hands.

Little did he know that he would spend eleven years writing checks to coaches, doctors, trainers, and physical therapists!

My parents were never happy that I devoted so much time to gymnastics. But, hey, my father instilled in me his determination and strong work ethic. It's my father's speed and strength and my mother's dance and ballet talent that ultimately gave me the skills to push deeper and deeper into the sport. They couldn't have known it when they got together, but Burt and Melanie Strug were made to be a gymnast's parents.

My dad is the most dedicated man I've ever known—more so even than Bela Karolyi or any coach or athlete I've met. People ask me how I kept pushing myself, never retiring from gymnastics even after a back injury that could have paralyzed me, a stomach injury that should have ended my career, and all those years in the shadows. People say I have a very strong will.

Well, if that's true, let me tell you where I got it.

When my dad was growing up in New Orleans, the grandson of Russian-Jewish refugees who landed in New York and later migrated south, people told him that he'd have a hard time duplicating his father's accomplishment of becoming a surgeon. He was born with a fractured clavicle on the right side of his body, which gave him a much weaker right arm. But even with restricted movement, my father accomplished his dreams. Growing up, he wasn't the biggest kid around, but for four years in a row he was voted the best all-around athlete in summer camp. In school, he played baseball and tennis, ran track, and even played football. Some of Dad's relatives say that he really was a good football player—fast and strong for his size (5 feet 5 inches). But he broke his weaker right arm twice in football, so my grandmother put a quick end to it and he concentrated on tennis.

Eventually, Dad landed at Brandeis University in Massachusetts, playing tennis for Bud Collins, who is now an NBC television analyst. He went on to medical school at Louisiana State University in New Orleans and continued playing tennis whenever he could. Even now, he still manages to squeeze in a match when he's not working, which isn't very often.

Dad has this great ability to throw all his energy into something and accomplish it, no matter what obstacles he faces. Like me, he's always been a meticulous planner. And if he decides he wants something, he usually gets it.

That's how he wound up marrying my mom, Melanie. He saw her once and decided she was the one for him. She was spending the summer with friends in New Orleans before her senior year. She met my father at a pool party and spoke to him for just a few minutes. The next day, he asked around, got her telephone number, and called: "Hey, remember me, Burt Strug?" They went on their first date, and just one month later, despite family protests on both sides, he convinced her to transfer to Newcomb College in New Orleans. Three months later, they were planning their marriage.

"If you ever do something that dumb for a boy," my father tells me, "I'll strangle you."

Dad loves mental and physical challenges. Even after medical school, he pushed himself to the limit. He earned admission into a cutting-edge medical specialty program in Houston developed by Drs. Michael DeBakey and Denton Cooley.

It was 1968 and Dr. DeBakey was setting the standard for cardiac surgery, the elite field my dad wanted to be in. Only twenty doctors a year were allowed into Dr. DeBakey's program, and after four years of training, only two of them earned the cardiac thoracic specialty. Fearing that his weaker right arm would be an insurmountable obstacle, friends and relatives advised my father to go into another field. In spite of it all, four challenging years later, Dr. Burt Strug was one of those two cardiac thoracic specialists trained by DeBakey and Cooley.

Under their training, Dad was on the front lines as bypass and transplant surgeries were developed. He trained six days a week, 5:30 A.M. until after 10:00 P.M., and was on call for twenty-four hours every other day. He lived in medical scrubs. He slept in vacant rooms at Methodist Hospital in Houston. With my sister, Lisa, just a toddler, my brother, Kevin, on the way, and money tight, Dad also moonlighted—literally—as an overnight emergency room doctor at various hospitals in Houston. My mother stayed with her family in Chicago for three or four months at a time while Dad worked practically around the clock. When she was in Houston at the small apartment they rented, she saw my dad for only a few hours on Sundays. Raising a young family with a resident doctor left Mom little free time, but she spent it practicing ballet. Dance was her first and lifelong love. For a while, Mom even studied with the renowned Houston Ballet.

When I got older, I talked with Dad a lot about those times. It must have been the hardest thing he ever did. When I was away from home myself, training and struggling, I found it easy to identify with the tough times he experienced. I thought about all the sacrifices we've made just so we could chase our dreams. He lived in scrubs. I lived in leotards. He slept in a hospital bed. I slept in cabin cots. We both woke up before dawn and came home after dark. We both chose paths that bruised and battered our emotions. Just like him, I devoted my life to fulfilling a dream and made many sacrifices along the way.

"In a sense, Dr. DeBakey was my Bela Karolyi," Dad told me once. "I wanted to train with him because he wrote the book and he was the best. I couldn't count how many times I got mad at him. I came home and punched a few walls, I was so mad. But the things we were studying and talking about back then were completely new and different. That drove me. I liked the challenge and the excitement of the competition. I never wanted to be defeated because death was a defeat. If you made it through that program, you were going to be fine."

It was tough, but my parents survived Dr. DeBakey's program. It was important not only because they accomplished their goals, but also because they knew that sometimes you have to be apart from someone you love who is chasing a lifelong dream.

In 1976, they packed up Lisa and Kevin and moved to Tucson to start Dad's practice. I was born a year later as the family was settling in to the new town and Dad was pushing himself to the limit getting his practice started. For years he worked at up to five different hospitals, performing an average of two to three open-heart surgeries a day and working from 5:30 A.M. until after 8:00 P.M. He usually left the house before any of us woke up in the morning and didn't get back until we were in bed. Only since 1996 have we convinced him to limit his workload, but he still works from seven until seven.

My father loves his practice dearly. Nothing stops him from fulfilling his dream.

Dad's big joke is that sewing has been in our family for generations. One of his grandfathers was a tailor; another worked in the garment district in New York. His father was a surgeon. "We've all sewn in this family," he tells me. "And you, Kerri, you *get* sewn."

Yes, long before my first competition I had a few scars already. I was practicing Kips—swinging from below the bar to the top—on the swing set in the backyard when I ripped open my knee on a screw. The scar runs from above my kneecap to the top of my shin. In first grade, I tried to do a front flip while jumping off a swing and busted open my chin. More stitches. I suffered a gash in my forehead running into the corner of a dresser and I have jammed and sprained my wrists and ankles so many times that Ace bandages were a regular part of the Saturday wash.

Lisa would ask, "Don't you get enough gym at practice?"

"Nope."

Not ever. My parents could see the trend of my injuries piling up at an early age. Even before I began competing, they wanted me to try several other sports.

They put me into tennis lessons—boring. I joined a swim team, but I could never find a swimsuit small enough to fit and I finished last in my first race. They took me skiing. I loved skiing and still do, but it's not exactly something you can do every day in Tucson. My mom signed me up for ballet, which was fun for a while. I participated in a few recitals and enjoyed wearing makeup. But I'm not exactly a tutu kind of girl.

Mostly I bounced around the house, copying Nadia, Mary Lou, or my sister. My parents kept our living room unfurnished until I was about six. Lisa, Kevin, and I took it over as a home gym. We called it the Green Room because of its shaggy bright green carpet. It was a big room, with a huge floor-to-ceiling mirror covering part of one wall. Lisa, who began gymnastics when she was six and has always loved the sport, practiced her moves there, and I was right behind her trying to do the same. I cried the day I came home from school and found that Mom finally got the room furnished.

"Where am I going to do gymnastics?" I asked. Lisa and Kevin were not pleased, either.

We three were always into something. And my poor mom was the one who sacrificed much of her life for us. With Dad working long hours and hardly home during the week, Mom carted Lisa to gymnastics practice, Kevin to baseball or gymnastics, and me to dance or gymnastics. Often all three of us had to be at different places at the exact same time of day.

Mom would race from one side of town to the other, dropping off and picking up. She'd frantically call Dad at his office. "How am I supposed to be at three places at one time?"

And Dad would reply, "Well, just pick one up early, one on time, and one late."

It got to be hilarious around our house sometimes. We did a lot of homework in the car. Most nights our kitchen was like a cafeteria, with each of us eating at a different hour. The ringer on the microwave oven was like our dinner bell. Sundays were great, though. On Sundays, we were together. Always. It was a family rule, in fact. Every third Sunday, each kid got to choose what the family would do. On the fourth Sunday, my parents planned the day.

My choice always was the same—Chuck E Cheese pizza! Yum. I played Skee-Ball until my arm got tired, trying to score points and earn prizes. It's still my favorite arcade game. I munched on pizza, ran around from game to game like crazy, and waited for Dad to say what he always did: "If you don't have a headache when you get here, you will when you leave."

We loved our Sundays. Our family has always been very close, even when we were far apart. As my parents learned early in their relationship, part of being close is loving each other enough to let go.

And Lisa was the first to move on.

She was an instant success in gymnastics and worked her way through the ranks, all the way to the Junior Olympics. The family went to watch Lisa perform in the Junior Olympics, and we were all so proud of her. Finally she earned an invitation to the National Academy of Artistic Gymnastics in Eugene, Oregon, where she trained under Dick Mulvihill. Among the future stars also training there were Tracee Talavera and Julianne McNamara. It was a great elite gymnastics environment, but it was in Oregon! My parents tried to talk Lisa out of it. Mom was pretty upset about Lisa's wish to move to Oregon. But Mom and Dad finally conceded.

I'll never forget the day she left in 1982. Lisa and I had done absolutely everything together. We had separate bedrooms, but nearly every night I sneaked into her room and snuggled with her. She had her own group of friends, but she still played makeup or dress-up with me every time I asked. When she had friends over, she was never embarrassed about her kid sister's tagging along. When we watched TV, I usually sat in her lap. She called me "baby" and "runt." She taught me how to do back handsprings and walkovers in her bedroom and made me feel better when I banged into a wall or a dresser. When she went to gymnastics practice, she took me along and stayed late so I could play in the pit, the big landing area with lots of cushions.

Lisa also had the personality I always wanted—outgoing, bubbly, able to walk into any room and make friends. She's always laughing about something. And she and Kevin are both much tougher than I emotionally. When one of us did something wrong, Dad would raise his voice and punish or ground Lisa or Kevin. Usually they just took the punishment as it came and went on. But all my dad had to say was "Kerri, I'm disappointed in you," and I'd burst into tears.

Basically, I was shy, almost a recluse. I internalized everything and never let anyone outside the family know what I was thinking. That part of my personality haunted me for a long time, and I've only recently been able to overcome it.

The night before Lisa left for Oregon, I clung to her like a baby. I slept with her as usual and made my mother and father promise to wake me up before they took her to the airport. But Mom and Dad decided it was probably best not to wake me. I cried for hours. I screamed at my parents like I never had before, "Why didn't you wake me up? What if I never see Lisa again? I can't believe you did this."

I was mad at the world. I blamed my parents for letting Lisa leave home and I blamed her for leaving. For weeks after Lisa left, I still slept in her bed with her dog, Suzy. I wrote Lisa lots of letters and drew her pictures. As time went by I got better about her being away, but I was still happiest only when the whole family was together.

When we went to visit Lisa in Oregon, I always had one of my famous lists ready, even though I could barely spell when she first left. I'd tell her: "Okay, first we're going to the movies. Then we're going to put on makeup. Then we're going to make some bracelets. Then we'll go out to eat pizza. Then we'll stay up talking until midnight." And so on. I brought those lists along every time we visited, no matter where Lisa was training. Even now when Lisa visits me in Los Angeles, I have a list of to-dos ready for her!

Back then, Lisa was a hard worker and was committed to gymnastics, briefly chasing an Olympic dream herself. She did great that summer in Oregon. When she went back two years later, my parents let me go with her. I wasn't training, just sort of tagging along as usual and participating in the gymnastics summer camp for kids. I think I got to go because my parents didn't want another scene like the first time Lisa left.

I really had a great time that summer. It was just Lisa and me together. And I learned a lot about gymnastics and the commitment it took to reach a high level. I saw how the girls lived together, slept in bunk beds, ate together, wrote letters, and coped with being away from home. I saw Julianne and Tracee right there training with Lisa. I still have the picture of me standing with Tracee that Lisa took.

In 1983, Lisa went to Bela Karolyi's gym in Houston for the summer. My parents weren't sure about Bela at first, but it was what Lisa wanted. One of the coaches assisting Bela was Steve Nunno, who later moved out on his own to Oklahoma City, where Lisa also trained later. At Bela's, the atmosphere was terrific, with my sister training alongside Mary Lou Retton, Dianne Durham, and Beth Pope. On a visit before Mary Lou's great performance at the Los Angeles Games, I got to watch practice a lot. I was amazed at all the tricks Dianne and Mary Lou could do. I don't really remember Bela or Martha from that trip. There were lots of coaches around and I was more intent on just watching the girls do their gymnastics.

I even tried some of the more difficult moves. Lisa would spot me on the hotel bed every night. At the gym I bounced around all over, practicing some of the same tricks the elites were doing. I wasn't even seven yet.

At the end of that trip, Gisi Oltean, an assistant coach who defected from Romania about the same time as Bela and later opened her own gym, cornered my father and asked questions about me. "Dr. Strug, your little girl has the perfect body for this sport," she said. "In Romania, it is not unusual to take these little ones and send them to a gym. She can get a good education here and become one of the best in the world. She is flexible and strong. She jumps powerfully. She is perfect to get started. I hope you think about sending her here. We'll take very good care of her and make her a champion."

My father responded, "Absolutely not," and turned and walked away.

While Lisa was at Steve Nunno's gym in Oklahoma City, an eight-year-old named Shannon Miller was beginning her career there. Steve also asked my parents about me. A year later, when I spent the summer with Lisa in Oregon, Dick Mulvihill tried to convince my parents to let me stay.

Suddenly I wanted to get more involved. All of these people kept telling my parents that this was something I should try. After all, Lisa was good at gymnastics and I loved the sport, so why not?

I knew what I was getting into. I know Lisa's gymnastics career could have been a great one if it hadn't been for injuries and her decision to become a normal teenager. Over the course of her career, Lisa had a compound fracture of her left elbow, a stress fracture in an ankle, and a stress fracture in her back.

The injuries piled up, and Lisa understandably lost some of her motivation. As she got closer to finishing high school and was in a position to earn a gymnastics scholarship to UCLA, she changed her focus to include things outside the sport, which had prevented her from having a social life for years. Kevin, who is two years younger than Lisa, also earned a gymnastics scholarship, but turned it down in order to pursue his dream of becoming a computer analyst.

Still, I wanted to compete. A social life? Hey, I was shy anyway.

The summer before my eighth birthday Mary Lou wowed the world with an individual gold medal in the all-around competition at the 1984 Los Angeles Games. Watching her affected me deeply. I had tapes of those games and I watched them over and over. Lisa bragged to her friends that I could name every member of the 1984 U.S. women's gymnastics team, and give every score on every apparatus.

She'd say, "Hey, Kerri, Kathy Johnson. Beam." And right on cue I'd respond, "9.85, bronze medal."

"Okay, Julianne McNamara. Bars."

"9.95. Tied for gold with Yanhong Ma from China."

I never missed. Even now I remember the members of the 1984 team by heart: Kathy Johnson, Tracee Talavera, Mary Lou Retton, Julianne McNamara, Pam Bileck, Michele Dusserre. The alternate was Marie Roethlisberger, whose younger brother John became one of the all-time U.S. men's gymnastics greats.

I wanted so much to be like one of those girls. It wasn't visions of glory and stardom that captivated me. It was the competition, and the spectacular tricks. I really believed I was born to do this sport. My dad was 5 feet 5, my mom 4 feet 11. I wasn't going to be a tennis player or basketball star. I knew I had some ability because people constantly told me I had the right body and the physical makeup. I was already doing stunts and skills that were considered advanced for my age. There was nothing I wanted more than to compete. Because of my sister, I'd already had a glimpse of what it took to reach the elite level, and I felt I could be myself inside the walls of a gym.

And all the gymnasts on television looked just like me. Nadia was so thin and small, with pigtails and all that bounce. Because of her I'd been wearing pigtails for years.

They were all real to me—not just images on the television screen. Maybe I'd never make it to the Olympics, but I didn't care. I wanted to compete. This was something I knew I could do and I wanted it more than anything. Nothing and no one was going to stop me from trying.

2

"Do you really want to do this?"

❁

I lay on the examining table and told the nurse that I felt sick to my stomach. She gave me a tray and I held it in one hand, my mother's hand in the other. The pain in my chest and stomach was unreal. I tried not to sob because it hurt so much every time I took a breath.

Mom and I looked at each other and I could tell she was thinking, "Please tell me you don't want to do gymnastics anymore."

Her worst fear had come true. I was not quite ten and had been preparing for the first big-time meet of my life, the Junior B American Classic. In practice I fell short trying to complete a Pike-Tsukahara. The Pike-Tsook is a common trick on the vault now, but in 1987 not many juniors were doing it. I went barreling down the vault runway, planted both feet on the springboard and did a half turn up to the horse, like a round-off. I pushed off my hands a little too late and couldn't finish the back 1½ somersault.

I jammed my head into the mats and my chin planted deep into my chest. I felt a pop and lost all my wind.

I shouldn't have been surprised that I hurt myself. I had been going all out for weeks, pushing a little bit more every day, because the American Classic meet was just two months away.

And on top of that, the meet would be held in my home state of Arizona, just up the road in Phoenix. I wanted to be at my best. I was training with Jim Gault, the University of Arizona gymnastics coach who months before had begun private lessons with me and Rose McLaughlin, a really talented gymnast two years older than I.

Before joining Mr. Gault, I competed for almost a year for the Gymnastics Center in Tucson, coached by Ellen Hinkle and Don Gutzler. From the first competitions, I was amazed at how much fun and success I had and how quickly I added difficult tricks. I beat a lot of girls older than I, although I didn't have a lot of blue ribbons. In most meets, Rose edged me out for first place.

Actually, Rose was one of my biggest supporters and always told me how far ahead of the game I was. She taught me a lot. Later in that first year, when I had caught up with her, she was still a great friend.

I also started doing advanced optional routines, winning many competitions. I was just eight when I went to the Class III state meet at Arizona State University and finished first in the nine-to-eleven age group.

I'll never forget that Class III meet because it was the first time I got a score of 9 from judges. I thought, "Wow. A 9!" At that time the gymnastics ladder included Class II and Class I levels, before reaching junior elites. After Class I was Junior B Elite and then Junior A Elite, which usually included the top twelve- and thirteen-year-olds. I began competing in Class III, but was advancing my routines so quickly that I skipped the next two levels and went right into junior Bs the next year.

I could do a standing layout on beam and a double-full somersault on the floor. I felt great. People I didn't even know came up to me after meets and said, "Hey, you were awesome today," or "We'll see you in the Olympics someday, huh?"

I usually smiled, bit my bottom lip or a callus on one of my hands—both bad habits I've never been able to shake—and thought, "Yeah, right."

Still, it wasn't long before Mr. Gault, a terrific coach of the fundamentals and proper technique, heard about me from another gymnast's parents. Kirstin Jones was a very talented girl competing in the Tucson area at the time. Her mother, who also was a gymnastics judge, approached Mom after a meet and told her that I should have a top-level coach.

"Kerri's too talented to stay where she is," Mrs. Jones said. "Let me call Jim Gault at the university and ask him to come watch her."

"He won't be interested in Kerri, will he?" my mother told Mrs. Jones. "She's so young. She's just learning."

"Oh, I think once he sees Kerri he'll be interested," Mrs. Jones responded.

And sure enough, Mr. Gault called, watched me work out, and took me under his wing. I began to realize that physically I was capable of doing difficult skills in gymnastics. Rose also joined Mr. Gault and we worked out with him three days a week, after he had coached his college team. We usually worked out from six to eight or eight-thirty at night.

Mr. Gault had a good coaching technique for someone like me. It included lots of positive reinforcement, which has always been good for me. He wasn't tough or mean, but he pushed us. We did good conditioning work and he was an expert teacher. Most days at the University of Arizona gym, it was just like when I bounced around the house, cutting open my knees and running into dressers. I would excitedly ask Mr. Gault to help me learn something new, and he'd be right there helping me as I went headlong into the trick.

The day I crashed practicing the Pike-Tsukahara, it was just miscommunication between us. He thought I was doing something else and I pushed off too late. The next thing I knew, I couldn't breathe.

By the time we got to the doctor's office, my mother's face was white. When the doctor walked into the examining room holding a set of X-rays, he looked at Mom and said, "Kerri has a fractured sternum."

My mother passed out. Her eyes turned white and she just sort of slid to the ground. A nurse helped carry her out and the first thing I thought was "Oh, no. There goes American Classic."

It was the first major injury of my career and, like always, it came at the worst possible time.

"Can you take some more X-rays and make sure?" I asked the doctor. I was so dumb. Take more X-rays? He got this strange look on his face and shook his head.

"It's fractured, Kerri. It's going to be a while before you do any gymnastics."

"How long?"

"A couple of months, at least."

I was devastated. It was less than two months before I got back, but it took much longer than I thought. I figured I would miss a couple of days of workout and still have plenty of time to get ready for American Classic. But I missed nearly two weeks of school and could hardly get out of bed.

Every morning I rolled over onto my stomach, slipped one leg down to the floor, and then slowly slid down the other leg. Finally I stood myself up, holding on to the side of the bed. It really hurt. My parents thought that would be the end of my gymnastics career. But I could deal with the pain. It was difficult to breathe, and if I sneezed or coughed, it was horrible. I was out of the gym for six weeks. But my anger disturbed me more than the pain.

On the day of the American Classic, I was really upset about not competing. I made my mother drive me to Phoenix so I could watch from the stands, and I just sat there, simmering.

It was the first time I saw Shannon Miller compete. She was amazing—so technically perfect. She'd sail off the vault or beam and—stick—there she would be in the perfect finishing position, hands out, chin up, with hardly a wrinkle in the landing mat. Shannon was about a year older than I and she easily won the Junior B Classic. As we drove home, I wondered if I would ever be good enough to compete with her. That was one of the first times I compared myself with someone else—another bad habit that was almost impossible to break.

But as soon as I got back into the gym, I got over missing that first big meet. In the next two years with Mr. Gault, everything just kept getting better and better. I won a lot and I competed with the very best.

At the U.S. Classic the next year, when I was ten, I just missed making the junior national team. Even though I didn't perform my best, that meet made a big impression on me. I was on the same floor as Bela Karolyi and the senior-level girls that he later took to the 1988 Olympic Games in Korea, Brandy Johnson and Chelle Stack. I got their autographs.

I finally did make it to the Junior B American Classic in Oakland, California, in 1989. And I won just about everything—all-around, floor, beam, and bars. I won at regional meets and national meets. I competed in my first international meet at the 1989 Junior Pacific Alliance and finished third in the all-around.

The routines got more difficult and the little injuries easier to shake off. I kept working. I wanted to try new, more difficult tricks. I moved up to the Junior A Elites and won almost everything at the American Classic—vault, floor, and bars—while placing in the all-around and beam. It was at a Junior A Classic that I first competed against Amanda Borden and Amy Chow.

I traveled all over the country for meets and camps and loved every second of it. One summer I trained with Scott Crouse in Fort Worth on the recommendation of Mr. Gault. That's where I met Sunshine Smyth. She is three years older than I, but we instantly became best friends. She and I had a bond, a lot like the one between Lisa and me. I could be honest and open with her— still can. And she was a very good gymnast. After spending that summer together, we wrote letters, visited each other on training trips, and talked on the telephone. That was the same summer when I developed another lifelong friendship with Katie Rose, whom I met in fourth grade. Katie took it upon herself to help me get over my extreme shyness. Every time there was a party that fit into my training schedule, she'd take me with her, even though I usually didn't want to go. For years she took care of me like a sister. I talked with Katie about my dreams and with Sunshine about how we wanted to make the 1992 Olympic team and then go on to compete at UCLA and room together.

Yes, by the time I was twelve and winning many competitions, I was beginning to think about the 1992 Olympics. I was starting to realize that I had the skills to become an Olympian. But honestly, I wondered if Mr. Gault had enough time in his busy collegiate coaching schedule to get me there.

I appreciated everything Mr. Gault did for me. He was a coach and a friend of the family. He taught me a lot and we could really talk about everything, not just about gymnastics. A lot of times,

Mom and Dad had him over for dinner or to visit. He even drove me home from practice a lot. We'd talk the whole way and sometimes stop for hamburgers. Now tell me. How many elite gymnastics coaches would do that today? Mr. Gault really took a lot of the pressure off me and some of the strain off Mom, Dad, and Kevin, who taxied me around quite a bit, too.

I have to say right here: Kevin has been like my guardian angel for my whole life. Like Lisa, he never complained whenever my gymnastics career interfered with his life. He spent days driving me to and from school or practice and never complained. And I couldn't count the times he actually took me with him on his dates, or out with his friends. Looking back, I realize Kevin did those things because he supported me and knew I needed to experience the world outside gymnastics. On Friday night when I didn't have practice or training the next day, he'd take me with him to pick up his date and the three of us would go to miniature golf or the movies or out to eat. Even today, Kevin looks out for me, organizing and running my web page on the Internet. I always knew I had a great thing at home.

But the meet that convinced me that I'd reached another level in my gymnastics career, a level at which I needed more time in the gym than Mr. Gault could offer, was the 1990 Dutch Open, my first trip overseas and the first time I got to wear an official USA leotard. I remember sitting in my room just staring at that leotard, running my hand over the letters and thinking that someday I'd wear them in the Olympic Games. That leotard was dark blue, with red and white piping on the shoulders. I thought I was big-time.

Still, on the way to such a big meet, I wasn't getting the intense training I needed. Mr. Gault was gone the entire week before we left for Holland. I didn't blame him for not being there, but I wished he had been. He had to take his Arizona team to NCAA championships, which was understandable because his college team was his first priority. Meanwhile I had to go to Phoenix and train with a coach I didn't know, and more important, he didn't know me very well, either. Mr. Gault was pulled in a lot of different directions, with meets for his college team and all the practice time.

Mr. Gault did go with me to Holland, but I felt unprepared and intimidated when I got there. It was a top-level international meet. Some of the girls had actually competed in the 1988 Olympic Games for Romania and the Soviet Union, on the strongest teams in the world. I watched the Romanians and Soviets warm up and thought, "Wow. I saw those girls on TV!"

A few foreign reporters came up to me before the meet and asked me some pretty blunt questions. "Who are you? Why are you here?" one man asked.

"I'm Kerri Strug." I didn't know what else to say, so I just sort of shrugged my shoulders and bit my bottom lip. "I'm here to compete."

"Why isn't Kim Zmeskal here? Why did America send you?" Much of the world press knew Kim by then. She had already been christened the next great American gymnast.

"I don't know," I said. "I guess they just wanted me to come this time."

But although I was pretty intimidated by everything around me, I did really well in Holland. I finished third in the all-around, second on bars and beam, and third on the floor. I beat the Romanians. I beat one of the Soviet girls. I couldn't believe it when they hung those medals around my neck. I was wearing the red, white, and blue and I had medals hanging around my neck. For the first time I had kids asking me for my autograph. It didn't matter to me that most of those Dutch kids, like the foreign press, didn't even know my name one day before. It didn't matter that they couldn't pronounce my name. They were still asking.

"Hey, Kerri, Kerri Stroooog," they'd call.

I bounced over to them and signed away, practicing my autograph.

When I got home, I did a lot of thinking. I thought about the Olympics. I thought about how strong and prepared Bela's girls, Brandy Johnson and Chelle Stack, had looked at U.S. Classic in 1988. I thought about how unprepared I felt in Holland. I went to an American Classic meet a few months later and did really well again. I thought some more about my dream. I thought about how Mary Lou, Dianne Durham, and Lisa always looked so perfect and prepared at Bela's gym. I remembered when I competed at a Zone meet at Bela's gym. I walked into the gym and first saw Bela, who was vacuuming the floor.

I thought, "Oh my God, there he is."

He looked up and said in that thick Romanian accent, "Hello, little one."

I remembered how after I won that Zone meet, Bela came up, patted me on the head, and said, "Hey, you're a good one. Good job. Keep working."

But I wasn't working, at least not the way I wanted to. Sunshine kidded me about never wanting to quit practice. When we finished a workout with Mr. Crouse in Fort Worth, I usually stayed in the gym by myself, doing sit-ups, leg lifts, or chin-ups or practicing pirouettes. Sunshine would stand near the door in her warmups carrying her gym bag. "Kerri, come on. We're leaving!" At Mr. Gault's, there were times when he had to talk me into stopping practice. I was comfortable only in the gym. A lot of kids at school never heard me speak, I was so shy. I walked around looking like a scared puppy. I never let anyone know what I really thought. Ask me a question and I'd usually bite my bottom lip and shake or nod my head. I was myself only in the gym. I needed more. I was thinking about the Olympic Games.

Finally I got up enough nerve and waited for Dad to come home from work. I walked into the family room and just said it: "I want to train at Karolyi's."

"What? You're crazy," my mother said.

"I'm not kidding. I want to go to the Olympics. I want to go to Karolyi's."

My mother's face dropped. It was the same expression she had before passing out in the doctor's office when I broke my sternum.

Over the next few weeks I pestered my parents about going to Karolyi's. I made a list, of course. I outlined all the positives and negatives. All I had was positives. I told them that I wanted to be one of the best, so I should train with the best. I was a year ahead in school and still making straight As, so they knew I would keep up my schoolwork. My Aunt Ann and Uncle Don Mangold had moved to Houston, so they could keep an eye on me. Lisa had gone to Karolyi's, so my parents already knew what kind of coach Bela was. The Olympics were just a year and a half away and this might be my only chance to make the team. Mr. Gault's time was limited. Besides, I would be a high school freshman next year and NCAA rules would prevent Mr. Gault from coaching me. My parents let Lisa do it, so why not me? Everyone in our family has made sacrifices. Remember Dr. DeBakey, Dad? The Olympics are my dream. On and on I went, nonstop every day.

All I heard from my parents was "Kerri, we want you here with us."

But one night I overheard my mother and father talking. Their conversation went back and forth for a while: She won't be able to handle the workouts. Okay, maybe she will. She'll never make it by herself. Yes, she will. She's never been around so many great gymnasts. She's too shy. She'll be intimidated.

Finally I heard the line that sent a shiver up my spine. "If the child wants it and she's willing to sacrifice for it," my father said, "we have to let her go."

The next day Dad asked, "Do you really want to do this?"

They told me that since the holidays were coming up, I could go to Houston on a trial basis. If it didn't work out I could come home. I had just turned thirteen. My mother cried. She picked up the phone and called Bela's. Martha answered and they talked for a while before setting up a visit.

From that point in my career, when I left home to train, my parents' demands never changed. Dad called it the triangle—the gym, the school, and the host family. They all had to be equally acceptable and supportive of the ultimate goal. Home schooling and correspondence courses were unacceptable. Living with the coaches was unacceptable. And why go elsewhere at all if the gym was not one of the best?

I would tell any young gymnast or any athlete, male or female, to follow the same rule. Don't ever compromise the triangle. The times when I broke the triangle, it nearly broke me.

After visiting Houston, my parents decided the triangle would work. I would stay with the Thompson family, who lived five minutes from Bela's gym. Jennie Thompson was a top gymnast, about four years younger than I. She also trained at Karolyi's and her parents were very involved. The school was Northland Christian, a good one that could accommodate my gymnastics schedule.

And the coaches were Bela and Martha. The best.

It was December of 1990. That Christmas, I asked for a diary because I knew Mom wouldn't be there for me every day when

I got home. She wouldn't be there to listen to me talk about my dreams and help me sort out my troubles. Just before leaving for Houston, I opened the diary and wrote: "Well, it's Christmas Day. I'm moving away for gymnastics. I decided I needed to write down my thoughts to you. I hope I'm doing the right thing."

I was petrified and thrilled at the same time. I had no idea how much pain and pleasure I would experience from that point on. I had no idea how many turns my life would take over the next seven years. Writing in that diary and the diaries that followed was like talking with Mom, Dad, Lisa, Kevin, Sunshine, Aunt Ann, Uncle Don. During the hard times, my diary became my therapist, psychologist, doctor, and friend. It helped me make it to a dream.

3

"What about the new girl?"

❦

I was in absolute awe. I had been in Bela's gym before, but as I looked around the place on that December morning in 1990, I realized that I now was one of Bela's girls.

For years, the entire world referred to the elite team from Houston coached by Bela and Martha Karolyi as Bela's girls. These were the select few gymnasts who marched into stadiums and arenas behind the big man with the bushy mustache, the man known for making friends, enemies, and Olympic champions.

While some considered it bad to be one of Bela's girls, others considered it the ultimate distinction. Some gymnasts, judges, coaches, and sportswriters despised Bela, calling him abusive, manipulative, and exploitive. Others considered him solely responsible for lifting American gymnastics to the top of the world. Bela's supporters called him an innovative genius, a man who adapted the Communist-bloc sports philosophy so that it would work in the free world.

As I looked around Bela's gym that morning, I honestly didn't know what to think. The gym wasn't at all like what some people might imagine. By the time I joined Bela, he had trained nearly thirty Olympians. His teams had won medals in every Olympiad since 1976. But his gym wasn't some sort of gymnastics

Taj Mahal. It didn't have mirrors on every wall or shiny and sparkling equipment like those fancy health clubs you see on TV. There were no beautifully framed and autographed pictures of all the stars he had trained.

It was more like a nice but simple workplace, a gym with a few banners hanging from the ceiling, posters of Mary Lou and Nadia stapled to the walls, and good but obviously well-used equipment. The air inside was kind of stuffy and smelled like chalk and sweat. The floor was hard. The locker room was nothing fancy: no plush carpet, spa, or steam room. It was just a dressing room, with a few lockers, some cubbies, and showers.

And looking at it all, I was in awe *and* scared to death. I knew that this big steel building off a busy farm road in North Houston was the place where I would finally get the work and coaching I wanted. It was simple and wonderful. My parents had warned me that my stay at Bela's was on a trial basis. But as I looked around, I decided I was not going to leave until after the 1992 Barcelona Olympics.

I had talked with Lisa and others about what to expect. I had experienced the life of an elite gymnast firsthand. But I missed Mom and Dad already, and neither had even left Houston yet. I had just turned thirteen.

I was so young, perhaps too young. Gymnastics was coming under more and more criticism for turning to younger, more limber athletes. But even then, I knew what I was getting into. I had heard what people were saying about girls who left home to join an elite gym. But the critics were wrong.

Had they seen me walk into Bela's gym that day, only 4 feet 6 and barely 70 pounds, they would have had a field day, I'm sure. With my hair pulled back into a ponytail and wearing a baggy T-shirt, I'm sure I looked scared to death. The critics would have gone through the whole routine: Supposedly Bela and Martha exploited wide-eyed dreamers like me. How could they be allowed to steal away my youth? Why did my parents let me train with a man famous for his tough coaching style? My body was going to be abused by the eight-hour days of training and pounding in the gym. My physical development was going to be damaged. My mind was going to be manipulated. I was going to be ridiculed and pushed too far and suffer permanent emotional damage. I was going to miss out on all the things young girls should experience: school dances, pep rallies, pizza parties, boys, family outings, three-day weekends, holidays.

I had heard all of this a thousand times by the time I walked into Bela's. And I would hear it again and again over the next several years.

But my dream was worth putting up with all the criticisms and risks. Leaving home for Bela's gym, or any elite gym, was not for everyone, but it was right for me.

Some people said elite gymnasts were too young and impressionable to be thrown into such a life. I thought that saying such a thing was discriminating against me because I was female.

I had been introduced to gymnastics by my sister and fell in love with it. My parents gave me every opportunity to improve. My first coaches pushed me because they saw I had talent. As a result of all that, I was embarking on the toughest trip yet on the way to my dream.

So how was that any different from the thirteen-year-old football player who smashes his body into blockers and spends six hours a day training and lifting weights? How was the so-called manipulation in gymnastics different from all the Little League moms and dads screaming at their kids from behind the backstop, "You blew the game, son"?

How was my leaving home at thirteen to follow my dream any different from young amateur boxers traveling all over the country to fight hundreds of fights a year? How were Bela's tactics different from those of youth basketball coaches? And how was the encouragement I received when I was three years old any different from Tiger Woods's father putting a golf club in Tiger's hands at the same age and developing a champion?

It wasn't. But the critics thought it was different because I wore my hair in a ponytail and stood 4 foot 6. That's sexism.

Still, Bela and Martha aren't perfect. It was hard to leave my world and enter theirs. And that's exactly what you do when you go to Karolyi's. You enter their world.

Yes, there were times when I disliked being around Bela and Martha, when they really got to me and I wanted out. I hated some of what they did and said, how they sometimes treated me and the other girls.

But I also loved them. Even before I earned my first world championship or made my first Olympic team, I loved that Bela and Martha made me better. I loved the way they took care of me and protected me. They are good people. But they are people from a different world, where a different approach was used not just in gymnastics, but in life.

Bela met Martha in 1965 at a gymnastics school in Onesti, Romania, where Martha was a young champion and Bela first coached. Sports was a big part of both of their lives. Soon, as Communist leaders turned Olympic sports into propaganda, sports became their entire lives.

Bela worked hard climbing the political ladder in Romania. He put up with a lot of backstabbing and a constant uphill climb in the Romanian sports system. When they first opened a gymnastics school in Vulcan, Romania, Bela and Martha made a lot of their own equipment out of old wood and boxes. They borrowed mattresses from the townspeople for use as landing mats. There was no money for leotards or sweatsuits, so the athletes trained in their underwear and T-shirts. Bela and Martha built their program by traveling about the area searching the schools for talented girls.

That's how Bela found Nadia. She was doing cartwheels on a school playground. Bela and Nadia were the start of a gymnastics revolution around the world. They were also the key elements in a Romanian gymnastics machine that for years would dominate the world.

But even after 1976, when Bela coached Nadia to the first ever score of perfect 10 in an Olympic competition, he received few privileges inside Communist Romania. All he knew was a confined life like nothing we could imagine in the United States.

An example of the tremendous pressure Bela felt under Communism was a horrible incident after his triumph in the 1976 Olympics. He is an avid hunter and was invited on a hunting trip to the Romanian national wildlife preserve by Romanian President Nicolae Ceausescu. This was a great honor for Bela because generally only the president's family and high-ranking government officials were invited to hunt in the preserve.

But the invitation was mostly for show. The president was to have a few pictures taken with Bela just to show the country that those who worked hard for the government could also have a privileged life.

Shortly before the hunt began, an official told Bela that he was forbidden to shoot any game animals on the trip. If Bela did shoot any, the official said, he would be severely reprimanded. Bela still went on the hunt "to enjoy the countryside and maybe shoot a rabbit," he told me, laughing. But soon Bela saw a black bear near where a forest ranger was leaning against a tree napping. When the ranger woke up, he startled the bear, who attacked the ranger. Bela lifted his rifle as the bear charged the man, but then he remembered the warning he had received and lowered his rifle. By the time Bela realized he could shoot his rifle in the air and scare away the bear, the ranger had been mauled to death. Had Bela shot the bear, the ranger might have survived, but the life that Bela had built for himself and Martha would probably have been over.

"That was Romania," Bela told me. "That was my life."

This was the man I was joining in Houston. From another world.

Bela, Martha, and choreographer Geza Pozsar defected to the United States in 1981, while on an exhibition tour in New York. They just walked out of a hotel where the Romanian national team was staying. Bela and Martha left their young daughter, Andrea, in Romania. All they could do was hope that Andrea would be allowed to join them in the United States.

Bela, Martha, and Geza wandered the streets of New York for a while, knowing only a handful of words in English. Finally they got in touch with Paul Ziert, an old friend who had a gym in Oklahoma. Ziert helped them get to California, where Bela hoped to get a coaching job. Eventually Geza got a job in Sacramento and moved there, while Bela and Martha stayed in the Los Angeles area. Bela worked as a dockhand and spent nights sweeping out a bar and washing dishes. Bela and Martha learned English by watching *Sesame Street* on television.

After six months, Paul Ziert finally got them a job coaching at a summer camp in Oklahoma. Shortly after that, Bart Conner, Ziert's star gymnast, arranged a meeting with United States Congressman Bill Archer, who secured Andrea's release from Romania.

Finally Bela was asked to save a troubled gym in Houston. After struggling to pay the rent for a while, he finally bought the gym, growing its membership into the hundreds. Next came Dianne Durham and Mary Lou Retton, Bela's first American stars and protégées. Bela's name was back on top internationally, and American gymnastics was on the rise.

Still, even before Mary Lou stuck that unforgettable 10.0 vault to win the 1984 all-around gold medal, Bela had his critics, people who didn't like his style and the way he practiced his elites two and sometimes three times a day. But he was a dream maker.

Gymnasts of all levels kept coming to Bela's for training. Thousands of girls trained under Bela and Martha every summer. Bela eventually bought 300 acres of land in the Sam Houston National Forest and began to build his American Dream retreat, a ranch where he built the ultimate gymnastics camp. Bela added a ranch house and three new gymnasiums on the land, which is about 45 minutes north of Houston. The ranch has cattle, horses, deer, mules, and goats and is surrounded by deep piney woods that reminds Bela of the Romanian countryside. Besides cedar log cabins that Bela built himself, there are a swimming pool and a pond stocked with huge catfish.

For us, Bela's girls, the gym in Houston was our first training home. The ranch was an isolated spot where we moved during the summer and before major competitions.

Once I began training with Bela and Martha, I quickly found out that I was unprepared for the intensity and competition within the gym. There were eight of us in the elite group at first. Six of the other seven girls had a huge head start on me, having trained with Bela for a long time before I arrived. Larissa Fontaine joined the group at about the same time I did. At the first workout at the Houston gym, I looked around and thought to myself,

"Wow. They're all better than me." I was always comparing myself with others. While I had only one or two routines on bars, they all seemed to have three or four. While I was doing the handspring front on vault, they already were doing round-off entries, which is the handspring to the springboard that vaulters use on such tricks as the Yurchenko. That first night I wrote in my diary: "Kerri, you have a long way to go."

I was the runt of the group, no doubt. But of the eight girls I met on my first day, only four of us were still there when we went to World Championship Trials less than ten months later.

Chelle Stack, the 1988 Olympian whose autograph I got earlier, was the oldest in the group. I was really impressed by Chelle. She had guts. She was outspoken, making her opinion known even to Bela. Chelle had missed out on an individual medal in Seoul when she fell on one of her best events, the uneven bars. Worse, the USA team just missed winning the bronze medal in 1988 when an East German judge, Ellen Berger, took away five-tenths of a point on a technicality.

Bela never has forgotten or forgiven Berger's controversial deduction. The Americans' alternate gymnast, Rhonda Faehn, had stepped onto the podium to remove the vaulting board during a teammate's routine, which is against the rules. Only coaches are allowed on the podium during a routine. Berger deducted the half point, which meant the East Germans won the bronze medal instead of the Americans. Chelle was trying to chase away that bad memory when she went back to Bela's as a seventeen-year-old. But it didn't work out. Chelle left Bela's about five months after I arrived.

Larissa Fontaine was a lot like me, a junior just moving up to the top level and giving Bela's gym a try. She was from Chicago and, like me, was used to training by herself. She had a hard time adjusting to the hectic training schedule and suffered a few injuries, leaving Bela's after about five months.

Amy Scheer was talented and had a big heart. She always pushed herself hard in practice and had a great influence on everyone. Luck never was on her side, though. She got sick, then had a hard time recovering. About six months after I arrived, Amy finally quit gymnastics. She just packed her bags and left one day, although she stayed in touch with all of us.

More graceful than powerful, Erica Stokes was really good on the beam. One of Bela's assistant coaches had discovered her while she was attending a summer camp at the ranch. Her whole family wound up moving to Houston. She was solid all-around and a beautiful performer. But she had spent a long time training at Bela's, and a few injuries finally led her to move on. Erica wound up at Steve Nunno's gym in Oklahoma.

Like I said, Bela's was not for everyone.

The other three elites at Bela's in 1991 were Kim Zmeskal, Betty Okino, and Hilary Grivich.

Betty was long, lean, and beautiful. She would become one of the best in the world on the beam, but constantly struggled with injuries. Hilary saved me so many times with her sense of humor. Hilary was as wild and boisterous as I was quiet and reserved. If I was homesick or having a hard day, she always made me laugh or put things in perspective. At the ranch, we'd walk into the cabins after a hard workout and Hilary would say in a funny voice, "We are in *hell*," emphasizing the last word.

Kim was the clear leader of the group and one of Bela's favorites. She was powerful yet flexible. During training, she wasn't always the best of the bunch, but put her in a big meet under the lights and Kim would perform like a champion. That's what Bela loved most about her. She was a competitor. Even during those first few days in 1991, long before most of us made it onto our first national team, I overheard Bela telling a reporter, "That Kim, she wants to perform. She wants the spotlight shining on her. She says, 'I am the one. I am going to win. Watch me. Look at me, world.'"

"What about the new girl?" the reporter asked.

"I don't know about that one yet," Bela said. "Right now, Kerri is saying, 'Yes, world, look at Kim. Don't look at me.'"

I knew Bela's assessment was true. I was the quiet one in the background.

At the time I didn't care. I didn't think it would ever affect how I performed or how judges looked at me. I just wanted to make it through the first week. Then I wanted to survive the second week. Adjusting to two practices a day was difficult enough, much less getting used to Bela's and Martha's heavy Romanian accents and their demands.

To Bela and Martha, training was always a means to an end. The way we lined up in front of Bela before every workout, shoulder to shoulder, backs straight, chests out, just as we would before international judges. The way we went all out on every apparatus every day, or risked being thrown out of practice. The way we took breaks or got water only at specific times. Everything was precise and disciplined. The occasional verification, which was a meet-like competition within the gym, with real judges brought in by Bela. Even the way we spent time isolated at the ranch, living in cabins together, as we would if we made it to the Olympic athletes' village. It was all part of our training, all a test.

There was always something new to learn and not a lot of time to learn it, some sort of pressure to perform. There's a saying about gymnastics: If it was easy, they'd call it football. Every time I hear that saying, I think of those training sessions at Bela's.

Usually, the day at Bela's began before daylight, and the morning session was heavy on conditioning and compulsories. Bela really emphasized hard aerobic work. For twenty to thirty minutes, we'd run around the floor, doing squat jumps every few steps, then jumps into a half turn, then jumps into a full turn, then shuffling our feet, toes pointed. We'd run forward and backward, kicking our feet to the sides, in front of us, and behind us. We would stop and do six to eight sets of forty and fifty sit-ups—lying on our backs, then on one side, then the other. We'd get to the bars and do pull-ups with our hands in various positions on the bars. We'd hang upside down on the high bar and do sit-ups that way. What fun! We'd get to the vault and do dozens of timers, which are various kinds of jumps. Then we perfected our compulsory floor, beam, and bars routines. It was exhausting. Six days a week, sometimes seven. Twice, sometimes three times a day. It all depended on Bela.

We usually went to school from ten-thirty until two-thirty, then home for a nap before physical therapy at four-thirty. At Bela's, you always went to physical therapy. Even if nothing hurt a lot at the time, something would soon. Physical therapy always helped.

The afternoon training sessions were devoted to optional routines and learning new tricks. The workouts often were an hour longer than scheduled. The afternoon workouts usually ended about nine at night. After practice, sometimes you had a private lesson and worked on a specific move or routine. Sometimes you had choreography with Geza, who often shuttled in from his gym in Sacramento. I learned so much in a short time. What I did in Tucson was nothing compared with this.

On and on the training went, nonstop. And the closer we got to U.S. Championships and World Trials, the more Bela and Martha began turning up the pressure to perform with perfection. The 1991 World Championships were going to be the most important meet for all of us up to that point in our lives. The meet this year was in Indianapolis and we all wanted to do well in our home country. And Bela wanted to get his girls back on top of the world, after disappointing results in 1988. The World Championships were also going to be a good gauge for what to expect at the 1992 Barcelona Olympic Games. Traditionally, the team and individual that wins a world championship the year before an Olympic competition is the favorite going into the Games. We all put up with everything we could as the 1991 U.S. Championships and World Trials approached.

On February 13, 1991, I wrote in my diary: "Things have been okay. Chelle's heel is not fractured, so she's probably going to American Cup. Amy is still out. Larissa has hyperextended her elbow and I'm hurting all over. My back is sore, my stomach has a pulled muscle, my heel is bruised, and my legs are really sore. But I'm doing well, even though everything hurts."

The more I learned in the gym, the more I wanted to learn. Of course Bela and Martha were tough, but we were in training. Bela simply challenged you to make every part of every routine better. Raising his voice, he would tell you what you did wrong. Or he would turn away shaking his head, and you knew it was time to try again.

Martha had her own way of getting to you. Her specialty was the beam. Bela spent hardly any time coaching or even helping Martha coach the beam. Often he'd leave the gym altogether and come back only when we were finished. I happen to believe Martha is the best beam coach in the world. But she's also tough. One minute she would make you feel so good about what you were doing, and the next, with just one look, a stare, or a word, she'd make you feel like crawling under the mats. Beam was my least favorite and worst event, but that didn't matter to Martha. She still demanded perfection, and I'm grateful she did.

By the time we started entering competitions, I was solid on beam and bars and very good on floor and vault. But because we were working so hard with little or no rest, none of us were at our peak level of performance for every competition. I got fourth place all-around at the Alamo City Classic in February at my first meet with Bela. I got my first all-around score of 39 at the Buckeye Classic. I got to the American Cup and was exhausted. I didn't do too well. After the American Cup, which was in Orlando, we took a nine-hour bus ride to Atlanta for a mixed pairs competition.

When we got back to Houston, I was doing some conditioning drills and sprained my ankle badly. I was out three weeks and was really stressed out. On March 25, 1991, I wrote in my diary: "Today was the first time Bela was really mean to me. I couldn't do my routines. It was all mind games."

I got into trouble because I tried to practice hurt, which is different from practicing in pain. I hated sitting out after I hurt my ankle because all the other girls were getting more gym time than I was. When I forced myself to train, I messed up. Bela blew up at me.

Bela and Martha quickly figured out that I didn't respond well to harsh criticism. Kim, Betty, and Hilary could handle it. If Bela blew up at them, they would just get mad and nail the next routine. It was as if they were saying, "Take that, Bela." But if Bela blew up at me, I became tentative and sad. I'd go to my room and cry. I began to think that Bela and Martha had no confidence in me.

But once I got healthy after that first bad injury, I still managed to become one of the strongest girls in the gym. I consistently won the verifications. But then Kim or Betty would win at the meets. I began pushing myself harder and harder, thinking that more practice would get me over my nervousness at meets. I knew I had become good enough to be one of the best in the world. I was always great in practice. Bela, Martha, and the other girls knew it. But no one else did—particularly the judges. We had a media day a few weeks before the U.S. Championships and I heard Bela talking about me.

"That Kerri, she's so strong, like a spark plug," he said. "Technically, you could not ask for a better one. Her body constitution is great. She is so strong and sturdy. But she needs confidence. When you tell her, 'Kerri, come on. Kerri, let's go' . . . when you start getting excited and want to fire her up, get her going, she pulls back like a little bird."

"Oh, great," I thought. "Bela called Kim his little lion. He called me a little bird. I hope this doesn't influence the judges."

The calls home kept getting longer and more frequent. Three-hundred-dollar-a-month long-distance charges were nothing. I kept counting the days until my next visit from Mom and Dad. Mom usually visited me once every three or four weeks, Dad a little less frequently because of his work. During the week, I counted the days until the weekend, when I could see my Aunt Ann and Uncle Don.

Those weekend trips into town to my aunt and uncle's house were lifesavers. Nothing I ever accomplished could have been done without Ann and Don. They lived on the west side of Houston, about forty minutes from the gym and an hour and a half from the ranch. Don joked with and encouraged me and Ann provided perspective and support. What also always helped were the long phone conversations with Sunshine and Katie. They will probably never know how important those talks were. And Katie, who sent me care packages of gum, candy, stationery, and other things from home, was a godsend.

The pressure of the upcoming U.S. Championships and world trials, the grind of the gym, was getting to everyone during those first few months. I don't know if I would have made it without Ann and Don. Chelle and Larissa were already gone. Amy was talking about quitting. Erica was soon on her way to Nunno's.

On April 17, 1991, I wrote in my diary: "I'm so homesick. I'm also sick and tired. Mom comes in on Friday and I can't wait."

I was calling home twice a day. I was sore everywhere. I'd have a bad practice and call Mom, crying to her, "I want to come home right now." She'd tell me she could be on the next plane if that's what I wanted. But then, I'd take a nap and start to feel a little better. I'd go to therapy and work out some of the pain and soreness. I'd think about how far I had come already and how close the championships and the Olympics were getting. I'd count the days until my next visit to Uncle Don's or the next visit from Mom. I'd write in my diary.

In late May 1991, I wrote: "Hello, how are you? I'm really tired and my shoulder hurts. My back is sore and my shins, too. We had a 6 A.M. workout yesterday. Fun, huh? Our afternoon practice went an hour and fifteen minutes longer than it was supposed to. That's not too bad, I guess. That's life. You know, we're really not too far from the goal. I guess I'll keep going."

I hadn't been home in six months. The 1992 Barcelona Games were thirteen months away. I knew I needed a lift and some balance in my life if I was going to keep going. My dad had talked about the triangle—the gym, the school, and the host family. The triangle was still working. I was still making straight As, competing in the gym, and getting along fine with the Thompsons. But I needed something else.

I realized that occasionally I needed to step outside that triangle if I was going to survive. I needed some sort of a life outside of gymnastics. I started calling Sunshine more often, talking with her about anything but gymnastics. During my weekends at Uncle Don's, I became a movie freak, sometimes watching as many as three in one visit. I took up arts and crafts—painting T-shirts, pottery—and started reading all sorts of magazines and books, immersing myself in the stories and escaping to another world even if it was just for a little while.

I would advise any elite athlete and that athlete's parents to come up with some version of the same thing. Get a life outside your athletic world. I have always been bothered by those parents who pick up and move everyone and everything to another city, just for the sake of their child's dream. To me, that's too much. Not only are you telling your kid that his or her whole life should be whatever the sport is, but you're telling him or her that all of your lives are devoted to that sport too. Talk about pressure.

My parents always told me that I should consider my Olympic quest like going off to college. I think that's a good way to approach it. They said that I should devote myself to it and work hard if that's what I really wanted. I should commit to doing whatever it took to accomplish it. But I could come home at any time and nothing would be different. If I got my degree, the Olympics, great. If not, I would still have had the experience of giving it a shot and I could move on to something else.

That being the case, on June 6, 1991, I was thirteen months away from earning my Olympic degree. In the nearly six months since arriving at Bela's, I'd learned that I had what it took physically. I'd put up with all the pain and training. I was being tutored by the best. I felt I was ready to join the world of Olympic hopefuls. Get my degree.

But U.S. Championships and World Trials were going to be my entrance exams.

4

"For regular people, today is a holiday"

❀

Tired and anxious, we were at U.S. Championships in Cincinnati, ready to take the first big step on the road to Barcelona. I know this sounds weird, but I decided that it was going to be a good meet for me when I went to the hotel gift shop and bought some Bazooka Joe bubble gum. I have always loved Bazooka Joe for two reasons. First, since we always were so careful about what we ate while we were in training, I figured that if I couldn't eat, at least I could chew. I chewed lots of gum. And second, because I am so superstitious, I get a kick out of reading the fortunes and proverbs printed across the bottom of the Bazooka Joe cartoon wrappers.

As we walked toward the hotel elevators after our morning workout on the day before Championships, I popped a piece of gum into my mouth and began reading the wrapper. "Success is limited only by your desire," it said.

When I got to my room, I opened my diary and taped that bubble gum wrapper to a page. "Well, tomorrow's the big day," I wrote. "I'll see if all my sacrifices and hard work have paid off. Success is limited only by my desire. Mom and Dad have arrived, but I haven't talked with them yet. I don't know if I want to."

Before major competitions I always keep to myself. I had to

enter my own private world before a big meet or else nervousness would ruin everything. I first realized how important focus and positive thinking were when I got to Bela's. Through all those exhausting days, "you can" and "you will" became regular entries into my diary. I became an amateur psychologist and I was my own best patient. As I pushed myself in training and my body hurt so much, I always told myself things like "Just a little more. . . . Push it one more time. . . . You've worked too hard to stop now. . . . You can and you will do this."

I also knew that I had to have the right attitude in order to handle the coaching styles of Bela and Martha. I didn't want to crumble under the pressure they put on me and the other girls. I wanted the pressure to make me better. I didn't want to wind up leaving, like Chelle and Larissa already had. Plus, I saw how well positive thinking worked for Bela. Attitude got him so far in life and made him a better person. Bela's favorite saying is "You can do it." When you really believe that you can accomplish something—I mean, really believe it in your heart—you usually can.

At U.S. Championships, I believed. I was nervous, but I beat the nerves. And I beat most of America's best gymnasts, too. It was my first major senior elite competition and I finished third in the all-around, third on bars, and first on vault. Kim and I tied for the best total all-around optional score. I couldn't believe it. I was national champion on vault, my favorite event. Sandy Woolsey finished second, Shannon Miller was third. Just a couple of years earlier, I watched Shannon compete and wondered if I ever would be good enough to compete with her. Now I had defeated her on vault. My performance helped my confidence and my standing internationally. Just weeks before the World Trials and a year before the Olympics, my name was placed among America's best.

At the press conference afterward, Kim Zmeskal, who won the all-around, got most of the attention. I sat there on the dais, holding a bouquet of flowers and looking at my medal. As usual, I looked nervous and shy, but I was very happy inside. I did eventually loosen up and answer a question about where I thought the U.S. Championships performance put me on the road to my ultimate goal. "Each meet is going to build to the Olympics," I said. "Every time you do well, it's going to help you make the team. Every time you don't, your chances get slimmer."

I got to see my family after the meet and we celebrated. Mom and Dad were so proud. And this was the first time I honestly believed that I could make the 1992 Olympic team. We talked about all the possibilities that the U.S. Championships meet had opened up for me, particularly about being ranked among the top gymnasts in the country. I could turn professional and earn up to $20,000 a year from the gymnastics federation. If I got an agent and a few sponsors and did some professional tours, I might be able to double that amount. But after discussing the possibility for a while, I realized that I didn't want to be a professional. That wasn't my dream.

"I still want to go to UCLA and compete," I told my parents. I wanted to keep my amateur status. My dad said he would inform the federation that I didn't want to accept the money. He kidded me about looking so serious during my routines and the interviews. "You should smile more," my dad said. "Show people that you're enjoying yourself."

He knew I was enjoying myself. I was just focusing on my routines. Some people criticized me for not smiling, but I was usually so nervous at meets that I could hardly keep my nervousness from affecting my performances.

In fact sometimes, no matter how hard I concentrated, nervousness *did* affect my performances. I knew that Bela, Martha, and maybe even my teammates were never sure how I would respond in a particular competition. Even after my great performance at U.S. Championships, Bela and Martha spoke to me about being more confident and not worrying about what other people thought of me. I thought that perhaps I should consult with a sports psychologist and try to come up with some more exercises in positive thinking. I knew I had to be ready for every possibility, physical and emotional, on the road to the Olympics. We hadn't even left Cincinnati yet and I was ready to get back to the gym.

But I didn't want to get back to the gym badly enough to give up the two short and wonderful days off we got after U.S. Championships. I went home for the first time in six months. My parents took me to all my favorite places and I visited with friends. I played with my dog Sandy in the backyard and walked around the neighborhood during those beautiful, cool Tucson evenings. I carefully hung my medals in my room. I spent time with Kevin and Lisa, both of whom were home from school.

The night before I went back to Houston, I got depressed. I begged Mom to come back to Houston with me. She told me she would be in Houston in a couple of weeks. I went to bed crying. I wanted to stay home, but I knew I had to leave because I wanted even more to make the Olympic team. World Trials were in two months.

When I got to Houston, Bela moved us all out to the ranch. School was out, so he said we were going to have six weeks of intense workouts. I thought to myself, "You mean, it can get more intense than it has already been?" During one of Houston's famous hot, high-humidity summers, we were working out up to eight hours a day. What fun.

Me at three, on vacation with my family. I couldn't walk past a curb without practicing my beam.

One of my first public performances, at a mall in Tucson. That purple leotard was my favorite.

My fourth birthday at
Chuck E. Cheese's,
wearing my favorite
Minnie Mouse dress.

Meeting Tracee
Talavera in Eugene,
Oregon, on my first
trip to visit Lisa.

Me at seven, performing at an exhibition in Oregon while I was spending a summer with Lisa.

At the Gymnastics Center during my first year competing. I was eight and into the pigtail thing, because I idolized Nadia.

One of the first times I ever saw my name in the newspaper, after winning the Reno Invitational when I was ten.

Sunshine and me in San Diego, vacationing with my family. I was not quite eleven. We always have been best friends.

At the 1990 Junior Pan Am Games in Tallahassee, Florida. We were
coached by Jim Gault and Kelli Hill, and I won the all-around.
That's Dominique Dawes to my far right.

On the beam in Holland at an
international junior meet when
I was twelve. It was the first
time I represented the United
States. I was so proud.

I could not believe it. My first senior national championship competition, and I won the vault. Sandy Woolsey was second, Shannon Miller third.

With Uncle Don and Aunt Ann at their home in Houston. It was my brother Kevin's birthday and also my parents' anniversary, which is why there are two cakes. Don and Ann were the big cooks of the family. They knew I had to be careful with what I ate, and they always came up with some creative and delicious low-fat recipes.

Backstage with Hilary Grivich and Betty Okino after winning the silver medal at the 1991 World Championships in Indianapolis—one of the happiest nights of my life.

At the 1992 USA Champs, with Michelle Campi, Hilary, and Kim. The two little ones (yes, even smaller than me!) are Jennie Thompson and Dominique Moceanu, future stars.

The four who survived Karolyi's and made it to the 1992 Olympic Trials—
me, Betty, Kim, and Hilary—in the locker room after a workout.

Bela and a lot of his girls, before the 1992 Barcelona Games. That's Nadia and Mary Lou to Bela's right. To his left is our choreographer, Geza Pozsar, along with (from left to right) Michelle Campi (who also once competed for Bela), Betty, Kim, Hilary, and me.

On the beam in Barcelona. I had such a good competition that I was devastated when I missed making all-arounds by .014 of a point.

The official postcard of the 1992 U.S. gymnastics team. We all got along fine, but after the turbulent Olympic Trials and selection procedures, it was difficult to become really close, like we would be four years later.

Me vaulting at the Olympic Sports Festival in San Antonio in 1993. When I first saw this picture, with me looking so skinny and my veins sticking out, I could not believe that I'd allowed myself to fall into bad eating habits and lose so much strength.

After my back injury in 1994, I went through four different types of back braces. The first one was very bulky. This was a neoprene support that I used after I began training again.

At practice, before the
DTB meet in Dortmund,
Germany. It was one of
the lowest points of my
life. I was in constant pain,
forcing myself to compete.
I could feel a divot in my
stomach. When I got
home, I found out I
had a severe tear in my
stomach muscle.

High school graduation at Green Field Country Day. It was great
to graduate from my high school in my hometown.

At the pre-Olympic training camp in Greensboro, North Carolina. Both my shins had been really sore at Olympic Trials and I had to keep them taped tightly.

Mary Lou visiting us at our pre-Olympic camp in Greensboro, North Carolina, in 1996. She's an incredible speaker, and I admire her so much.

One of my favorite pictures of Bela. He's with Martha, Dominique, and me just after we got to Atlanta.

I was the last one up on floor at the Olympic team finals, and the Russian team was still putting pressure on us. I had the routine of my life. I'll never forget it.

Compulsory beam never has been my favorite routine, but in Atlanta I was very confident. Thank you, Martha!

I'm completing a release move during our first event of the team finals competition in Atlanta. We entered the finals trailing Russia, but made up all the ground on our first rotation.

When I got through optional beam during the team finals, I breathed a huge sigh of relief. I felt certain I would make it to individual all-arounds.

anta 1996

From the moment we arrived in Atlanta, the attention and security that surrounded us were amazing. This is me boarding the bus on the way to team optional finals. I never, ever would have guessed what was going to happen that night.

Shortly after we moved to the ranch, my shins began bothering me so much that I had to get bone scans on them. Because I was so tired, I kept falling asleep during the procedure, which meant they had to start the tests over. After three hours, I found out that I had stress fractures—nothing too bad. Besides, I got to take a nice nap. I took it easy for a couple of days and then went back into the gym full speed.

As we worked more and more hours each day, life at the ranch soon became almost unbearably monotonous. I always did my best training when I knew there was something else, something outside the gym, that I could stay involved with. I always liked having something at the end of the rainbow each week—school or my arts and crafts, visits from Mom and Dad or to Ann and Don's. At the ranch, we were isolated from everything. Time ran together. The only date branded on any of our minds was September 6—World Championships. When Bela announced in July that we were no longer going to be allowed to leave the ranch on weekends, I found it harder and harder to stay focused during workouts. I knew this was all just Bela's constant testing, but I didn't like it.

Shortly after Bela's announcement, I hurt my hand pretty badly doing some simple moves on the beam. I was practicing flip-flop tuck kickouts—basically, back handsprings with a few variations—and jammed my hand on the side of the beam on a tumbling pass. I finished the workout thinking the pain would just go away, but my hand swelled up and was really sore. Bela looked at it and didn't say a word. I think we both realized that it was going to take some time to heal. The injury was definitely going to keep me from training for a while, and World Trials were only a month away. Once again, I was stressing out. Why was I always the unlucky one?

At least I could leave the ranch for a few hours. I needed to have my hand examined and Kim needed some treatment, too. Bela got a trainer to take us into Houston to see a doctor. But on the drive into town, we got brave. Maybe we were stir crazy from being confined to the ranch. But Kim and I begged, finally convincing the trainer to take a detour on the way to the doctor's office.

We went to Pizza Uno's! We knew that if Bela found out, he would kill us for sure. The one time Bela allowed us to leave the ranch, what were we doing? Going out for pizza—one of the worst things an elite gymnast can eat.

Usually, our diets at the ranch consisted of not much more than chicken, rice, and salads, over and over. We had no-fat dressings and no-fat milk, and our big treats were fruit bowls. Martha always kept close tabs on our diets. We weighed ourselves regularly and always tried to stay in a certain range while we were competing. The newspapers at that time were full of stories about elite coaches allegedly starving their gymnasts and causing eating disorders and bad eating habits. And there were—and are—such problems in the sport, I'm not going to deny it. But we had realistic goals that offered us the best chance to succeed during a time when international judges favored small bodies with big-difficulty routines.

The weight goals were different for each of us. And these goals were not unreasonable, considering our heights and the sport in which we competed. Kim was 4 feet 7 and powerfully built, with strong legs. There was no way she could compete at a high level unless she stayed within a certain weight range. Betty was 5 feet 4 and had a longer, more elegant frame than any of us. She could carry more weight and still compete at a high level. I was the smallest of all. My ideal weight at that time was about

80 pounds. Most of the time, we stayed within our ranges by eating chicken and rice and little fat in anything.

Most of the time, we could deal with the food at the ranch because on weekends we could eat something different. When we trained in town or could leave the ranch on weekends, we usually went to our families' homes—in my case, Ann and Don's—and cheated on our diets a little bit. Ann and Don would take me out for some frozen yogurt or treat me to some good pasta or maybe a lean steak at a restaurant. It always was a nice change and kept things lively.

The food at the ranch was getting to us as much as the practice. When we got to Uno's, we ordered a huge deep-dish cheese pizza and started munching. It was awesome. I love pizza so much. I was in heaven.

But all of a sudden a man walked by our table and said, "Hi, Kim. Hi, Kerri." It was a local sportswriter we all knew.

"Ohmygod, we're dead," I told Kim. "He's going to tell Bela and we're going to be dead."

"Yup, we're dead," Kim said. "We're going to die."

For a moment we stopped eating and talked about how maybe we should go beg the writer not to say anything to Bela. But then Kim picked up another slice of pizza and said, "Oh, forget it. Let's just eat. It will be like our last supper."

We decided we didn't care how much trouble we got into. Munching on pizza was worth all the running, sit-ups, and push-ups Bela would make us do. And as it turned out, everything was fine. The doctor said my hand was not broken and the writer didn't say a word to Bela. I saw the writer later and thanked him for not saying anything.

"Don't worry about it," he told me. "Sportswriters train on pizza, too."

I think the writers, team sponsors, and parents who were around Bela's ranch at that time felt sorry for us. They knew what we were going through to reach our dream. And they knew that as much as we all trained for the Olympics, the odds were against all of Bela's girls making it to the Games. Some of us were bound to be disappointed no matter how hard we worked.

With all the talk about Bela "stealing" our lives with the hard training, starving us, and putting too much pressure on us, Bela was looked upon by some as the bad guy. He had enemies in the gymnastics world. Other elite coaches resented Bela for all the attention he received. Some judges disliked him because he was never afraid to point out a mistake if he believed one had been made.

Both Bela and his girls knew that it was going to be difficult for all of us to make the 1992 Olympic team. That would be four spots on a seven-member team, and as strong a presence as Bela had in the sport, that was asking a lot.

So as the World Trials approached, the pressure started getting to us even more. We all wanted to prove that we were the best of Bela's girls. We began competing against each other. I tried to outdo everyone else in the gym, and everyone else was trying to outdo me. I really liked Kim, Betty, and Hilary, but I wanted to beat them. I realized that being considered the third- or fourth-best girl in Bela's gym was not going to help me get to the Olympics. Kim was the star, and the judges really respected her. The same was true for Betty. But where did that leave Hilary and me? I didn't want my reputation for being third best in my own gym to keep me from reaching my dream.

All of us were feeling the tension. Only four of Bela's girls were left. Erica went to Nunno's, saying she needed a change. She just walked into the cabin one day and started packing her things. "I'm not going to do this anymore," she said. That was it.

I knew I never would leave Bela's. No matter how much it got to me or how hard it was to get out of Kim's and Betty's shadows, I was going to stay. I knew I had to convince myself and Bela that I should be considered in the same class as Kim and Betty.

We had a verification before World Trials and I treated it like a championship meet. I was so focused. Bela invited the summer campers to come watch the competition and the little girls filled both sides of the gym, cheering. I didn't say anything, but I imagined that I was at the World Championships, in the individual all-around finals competing against Kim, Betty, the Soviets, and the Romanians. I even wore a USA leotard. And I won the verification. I asked myself again: Why was I always able to win when the contest didn't really count?

Still, physically I knew I was ready for World Trials. I think all of us were more than ready. We were tired of competing so hard against each other; we wanted to compete against someone else. I think we also realized how strained our relationships were getting, and we didn't like that. We were friends and needed to pull together.

And nothing pulled us together more than a big meet. At least we never carried our rivalries outside the gym. We always continued to get along great, I think because we knew not many teenagers in the world were going through what we were.

A couple of months after Amy left, we had a little episode that pulled us together. Amy came back to visit us at the ranch and we decided she'd spend the night in our cabin. We wanted to have a slumber party. Unfortunately, Martha, with her sixth sense, must have figured we were up to something. Martha walked into our cabin with Betty's grandmother, who stayed with us at the ranch. It was after ten-thirty at night and Martha rarely came to see us so late.

Amy heard Martha walking toward the door, so she jumped into the closet to hide. The rest of us had terrified looks on our faces, but we were determined to protect the big secret. I jumped up on my bunk as Martha walked in and opened my diary as if I had been writing in it all night.

For nearly forty-five minutes, Martha just stood there, chatting away with Betty's grandmother. "I hope Martha leaves soon, because I don't know what we're going to do if she finds out Amy is hiding in the closet," I wrote. "I hope Amy has enough air in there. I hope she can breathe."

Finally Martha said she needed to borrow some sheets, so she opened the closet. She really wasn't too mad when she found Amy, but Martha wanted to know whose idea it was that Amy spend the night with us. We all shrugged our shoulders. I think Martha knew all along that Amy was in there. She told Amy to go sleep with the camp counselors for the night, and that was that. We laughed about it for a while and went to bed.

"I think workouts are going to be tough tomorrow," I wrote in my diary before turning out the lights. "Oh, well, it was worth it seeing the look on Martha's face when she opened the closet. I'm glad I rested today."

By the time we got to World Trials, we were all thrilled to see any gym other than the one at the ranch. Once we began competing, we funneled all that energy into some awesome routines. It was such a team effort by the four of us. All four of Bela's girls made the World Championship team—Kim, Betty, Hilary, and me. Kim won all-around. I finished third. Bela was named head coach for World Championships. The other members of the USA's World Championship team were Michelle Campi and Shannon Miller, with Sandy Woolsey the alternate.

"This is going to be a great team," I wrote in my diary.

We went straight to Indianapolis after Trials and Bela began motivating and molding the seven of us into a team like only he can do. Bela is really good at figuring out the strengths and weaknesses of a team, *any* team. And he's the best at getting minds and bodies ready for a big meet. He made the seven of us feel unbeatable, even though we knew the Romanians and Soviets were thought to be better than us. But Bela called us tigers. At our workouts, he constantly encouraged, energized, inspired. After we hit a big routine at workouts, he gave us a big bear hug and shouted, "You're ready! You can do it, you can do it!" And by Labor Day 1991, we did feel like tigers. We were hungry and ready.

"For regular people, today is a holiday," I wrote in my diary. "We're going to work hard these last few days before Worlds and we're going to kill. We're going to win."

Well, we didn't win, but it was still the best nonboycotted international meet a U.S. team has ever had. All of our performances were incredible. We confidently walked into the Hoosier Dome and started hitting routine after routine. After every girl performed, Bela was at the bottom of the stairs, nodding his head—"Yes, yes, very good, you did it!"—and hugging us. Everything went perfect. We won the silver medal as a team, barely getting edged by the Soviets for the gold. We beat the Romanians for the first time ever, which thrilled Bela. Kim became the first American ever to win an individual all-around World Championship. Kim also took the bronze on the floor exercise. Shannon won the silver on the uneven bars. Betty won the bronze on the balance beam.

It was the thrill of my life. The atmosphere in Indianapolis and at the Hoosier Dome was crazy the whole week, with the crowd roaring in support of everything we did. We couldn't walk anywhere without signing autographs. Sure, I didn't quite meet all my goals individually, but I hit everything. I was thrilled. I had no complaints. I was only thirteen, the youngest competitor in the entire competition, and I had a silver medal from World Championships. The top thirty-six gymnasts individually qualified for all-arounds, but only three were allowed per country. Even though I finished in fifteenth place individually, Kim, Betty, and Shannon were three Americans ahead of me. Therefore, I couldn't compete in the individual all-arounds. I really wanted to compete for an individual medal, but I was sure that, being so young, eventually I would.

At the press conference after the team finals, I sat with Hilary to one side of the interview room, watching in awe at how Kim was handling all the attention. She looked like a world champion, so comfortable and confident. I was so proud to know her.

The final day of competition was Bela's birthday, and he and Martha were so happy with our performances that they actually gave us all a piece of cake and nonalcoholic daiquiris. Bela said we could even take a sip of champagne, but I didn't.

I left the party early and went to my room. I opened my diary. "What a great day for the USA!" I wrote. "One of these days, Kerri, it's all going to come together for you. You're going to reach all your goals."

I went to bed and stayed awake for hours, thinking about how far I had come and how close the 1992 Olympic Trials and the Barcelona Games were getting. I thought about how the only goals remaining were making the 1992 team, helping the team to the gold, and earning an individual medal. I pictured myself in Barcelona, making the individual all-arounds, competing against Kim, the Soviets, and Romanians. I couldn't wait to get back into the gym.

5

"No winner is predetermined"

❀

As proud and happy as I was at World Championships, as thrilled as I was to actually be training alongside Kim, the world champion, those feelings gradually began to disappear once we got back to Houston. It wasn't Kim's fault at all. Kim had earned everything she received and seemed unbeatable. She and Betty were both at least two years older than I and had a lot more experience. Kim had been training with Bela for eight years. I had been there for one. You could see the confidence Kim and Betty had even in the way they walked. This was especially true for Kim. She was the best in the world, and after winning the all-around, she even *looked* like a world champion. She just had an aura. She was my friend and I admired her so much. But I have to admit, I was becoming jealous.

I knew that every day at the gym, I competed as well as or better than Kim, but she had that something extra during meets. Whatever it was that made her so confident, I wanted it, too. As hard as Kim worked, I thought I worked harder. I never took days off. If I was injured, I usually just went to therapy, wrapped tape around whatever was aching, and tried to keep going through the day. Bela took me aside once in a while and tried to encourage me. He realized that despite the success I was having, I still constantly compared myself with others and worried about what judges and other coaches thought of me. He also realized I had the potential to perform even better than I had at the U.S. Championships and Worlds.

"Kerri, you have a different body type than Kim," he told me. "You have agility and catlike reactions. You can act so quick and explosive. You have a lot of muscle and a solid body. And when you work, sometimes you overdo it. You look sometimes like you are going to fly away. You will have your day, Kerri, very soon. You just have to be confident."

It had been only weeks since we won the World Championships silver medal. But the thrill of that accomplishment no longer sustained me. Bela was telling people that Kim's individual World Championship title was going to be worth a tenth of a point for her in every competition from then on. Kim was getting so much respect from the public, the media, and the judges that she seemed especially confident at meets.

I felt more pressured, and the more others tried to encourage me, the more pressure I felt.

I expressed my frustrations only to my diary, my family, and my best friends outside the gym. My mother could always feel when the pressure was becoming overwhelming. She'd call and say, "Kerri, I can tell by your voice . . . What's going on?" And we'd talk about how I was feeling, about how difficult it was to be younger and in the shadows of Kim and Betty. I thought I'd never become a "meet" performer.

Sometimes Mom would call Lisa at UCLA and tell her, "Call Kerri, she's feeling down." And Lisa would pick up the phone and call me, even if she had been studying for an exam or preparing for a UCLA meet. She always made things better. She'd ask me how I was doing and I usually answered, "Oh, I'm just my usual stressed-out self."

But by the end of every conversation with Lisa, I was ready to face another day. Lisa made me laugh about the things that worried me, relating a similar experience she'd had while training with Bela or reminding me how far I had come already. Sometimes Lisa would imitate Bela and Martha, which I never had the nerve to do even in private. "Bela and Martha? What do they know about you? They don't even know how to pronounce your name," Lisa would say. Then she would go into her Bela impersonation: "No, no, Kah-dee, Kah-dee . . . like dees, Kah-dee, like dees. Do it like dees."

I'd die laughing. Lisa was great.

One night around Christmastime in 1991, Lisa called and opened her heart to me. I was so touched and inspired. "Let Bela call you every name in the book," she said. "If he yells at you, so what? He just likes to yell. You know what you're capable of doing, Kerri, so do it. You can handle anything Bela throws at you better than any gymnast in the world. You can beat any gymnast in the world. Don't do it for Bela or anyone else. Don't worry about Kim or anyone else. Don't you still love gymnastics?"

"Yes."

"Well, just enjoy it! Kerri, everything always catches up to people. One of these days, it's going to be your day. My gosh, you're only fourteen! Even if you don't make this Olympic team, you'll be around and make the next one."

Then Lisa told me something I'll never forget. "Kerri, for me there came a point when I was able to let go of gymnastics and move on. It just got to be too much for me to keep going at that level. That's the difference between you and me. I could let go. You never have been able to let go, and I don't think you ever will until you get what you really want. Don't worry about what's happening right now. You're going to overcome everything. I know you'll reach all your goals. Just keep doing what you're doing. You're going to get there."

She was right. I never could let go of my dream, which was both a blessing and a curse, I guess. Not since I began competing did I want any more or any less than the same three goals—the Olympic team, a team medal, and individual all-arounds.

Christmas Eve was just six months before the 1992 Olympic Trials, and I wasn't about to let go of my dream. I knew I needed to stay involved in life outside the gym. I thought the best medicine would be to spend Christmas at home with my family. But that didn't happen.

Bela decided we needed to stay in Houston through the holidays in order to keep our training regimen consistent. It was the first time in my life I hadn't been home for Christmas, and I was so upset. At the gym, we decided to have the best Christmas possible, so we had a Christmas party after the evening workout on December 23. We drew names and exchanged gifts; I got Kim's name and she had mine. We had a little show, with skits and Christmas carols. We all laughed about wanting to do a skit making fun of Bela or Martha, but none of us had the guts to do it after what had happened the year before.

That was when one girl decided to tease Martha in a skit. The girl who played Martha told the elites what we could eat: "And for dinner, since it's Christmas, you get *two* grapes!" The skit was funny, but Martha got upset because gymnasts' eating habits have always been a touchy subject. We decided never to do another parody of Bela or Martha. After the party, we all stayed up until almost three in the morning and had a great time. But it wasn't home.

After dragging ourselves through a workout at eight the

next morning—yes, Christmas Eve was just another day at the gym—we had the afternoon off, so I went to Ann and Don's. We had dinner and I opened some presents from home. Then I opened my diary. "I'm over at Ann's feeling sorry for myself," I wrote. "I wish I was at home celebrating Christmas. I can't believe I'm not with Mom and Dad. I hope all the sacrifices pay off. I miss home."

By late January, Bela was ready for us to make the final push before the Olympic Trials and the Games. We were going to have a really difficult schedule, but Bela tried to get us into top competitive shape and then did whatever it took to keep us at that point all through the Olympics. This was probably not the best strategy. Within a span of three months, we were scheduled to do a couple of exhibitions and to compete in the American Cup and the World Championships in Paris; then we were going to be off to the U.S. Championships. Kim, Betty, Hilary, and I discussed the schedule, wondering if we were going to be able to perform at our best every time out. We had all chosen difficult routines. We all had a lot of aches and pains. The risk for injury was great. It was asking a lot to expect us to nail every routine every time out.

But we pushed on. We realized that all the years of dreaming and working were about to come to a head, for better or worse. For me, the effects of the pressure and tension began to surface in a new way. I became an insomniac.

On January 24, 1992, I wrote in my diary: "I was exhausted last night, but I lay awake in my bed from ten-thirty until nearly three in the morning. I woke up at five-thirty."

Three days later, I wrote about a similar bout with insomnia. A day later, I couldn't sleep again. I went on a nonsleeping jag, which was awful. I talked to my father and other doctors; they thought it might have something to do with my thyroid. Whatever it was, I couldn't shake it for a while.

In February, I wrote: "I haven't slept for the last three nights."

I had some tests done and the doctor said there was nothing wrong with me physically. "Just as I suspected," I told my mom on the phone that night, "it's all in my head. Now, *that's* just what I needed to hear."

I went to a sports psychologist, but I couldn't really open up to him. He would ask me how I felt, and I'd say, "Well, okay, I guess." Not exactly candid.

Bela and Martha were concerned but not worried, because I never let anything affect my workouts. I knew that I had to perform in the gym, so I always did.

One night on the phone with Sunshine, I asked, "What's going on with me? Why can't I sleep?" "You put too much pressure on yourself," she replied, "and you always want to be perfect."

I kept thinking to myself, "Oh, Kim and Betty are so good. Hilary's so good. I hope I hit today. I know they're going to hit. What if I don't hit? What do I have to do?"

Everything just started piling up.

But Bela gave me a lot of chances. He would say, "Okay, this is the meet, Kerri. This is the one you're going to hit."

We got to American Cup on March 6. I wanted so desperately to make individual all-arounds, to show Bela and everyone else what I could accomplish in a big meet.

Unfortunately, after I hit everything so strong early and was in the hunt, I faltered on my final event, the floor. I had done it again: I *almost* got there, but not quite. I finished less than two-tenths of a point away from making individual all-arounds. This time only *two* Americans were allowed into individual all-arounds, and my scores were third best among the Americans.

Disappointed again. Kim wound up winning and Shannon was third. Kim was terrific. Not only did she win the all-around, but she won vault and floor. Bela told me I did fine; it was just lack of experience that kept me out of all-arounds.

I wrote in my diary that night: "I'm sick of always being the alternate or finishing third. I'm ready to move up. Maybe it's not my turn yet. I'm waiting for the World Championships in Paris, the U.S. Championships, the Olympic Trials, and the Olympics."

I always encouraged myself by saying things like "Okay, forget this meet. You'll do it at the next one!"

The next one was the World Championship Challenge in Paris, and I did well. However, I was interviewed before the World Championships and some of my comments were taken out of context. Anyone in gymnastics already knew the story: I was the young underdog in Kim's shadow. I was great in work-outs and good in meets. I had lots of potential.

When a reporter asked about my place behind Kim and Betty, I responded, "Kim has done so much in the past couple of years that people put her above the rest of us. She deserves to be there, but sometimes I feel like saying, 'You know, I'm here, too.'"

Later, ABC came in for some interviews and I told them that I thought I was as good or better than Kim in the gym. I also said that Kim had great mental toughness, and that's what made her a champion. But when ABC aired the interview, they edited out most of what I said about Kim's mental toughness. Kim just heard me say that I thought I was better than she—not the best thing for her to hear.

We had a verification before the U.S. Championships and Kim didn't do as well as she normally did. I won. Afterward, I tried to encourage Kim and told her, "Don't worry, you'll do well in the big meet."

"I know," she said. "You've already told the whole world."
I was shocked and intimidated. I felt horrible.

A few days later, Leslie Spencer, one of the trainers at Karolyi's, could not have picked a better time to give my confidence a boost. Leslie could see how I was being affected by Kim, Bela, Martha, everything. She clipped out some articles on motivation and confidence and keeping focused. She handed me the articles and included a handwritten note to me. I taped the note to a page in my diary and still consider it a prized possession.

"Kerri, I just want to impress upon you the fact that *anyone* can win," she wrote to me. "You have remarkable talents and every ability to win. It is important that you allow yourself to know that. I'd hate for you to look back on your life and wish for the opportunity again. I would hate for you to wish you had another chance. You only get *one* chance. Make the most of it.

"No winner is predetermined. Everyone has equal opportunity. *Anything* can happen to anyone at any time. You will never know what is in store for you. It could be something great. Please allow yourself to accept the fact that you are as deserving and great as the rest. If you let others intimidate you, you are only allowing them to keep you down. You are only allowing them to keep you from reaching your potential. Medal or no medal, as long as you do your very best and know that you've given it your all, you will always be proud and satisfied. You will always be able to look back and have no regrets. That, too, is very important."

In May I went to the U.S. Championships, which was the qualifying meet for the Olympic Trials. Of all things, the vault let me down on the first day. Still, I started the second day in fourth place and in good shape.

Only the top fourteen athletes were going to qualify for the Olympic Trials. Shannon won the first day's competition, but she was recovering from a dislocated elbow and was competing only in the compulsories. Betty had a stress fracture in her back and couldn't participate. Those injuries, and one suffered by Michelle Campi before Trials, would lead to controversy at the Olympic Trials in June and would also play a big part in the 1992 Olympic team's never really becoming the close-knit, unstoppable force that the 1991 World Championships team had been.

Kim wound up winning U.S. Championships—her third consecutive national title—and I had a great second day and moved all the way up to second place. I had the best bar routine of my life, had a strong beam, and hit a great vault for a 9.9. In the event finals, I won vault, tied for first with Kim on beam, and finished second behind Kim on the floor. Great! We were all so thrilled. Sunshine sent flowers to my hotel. My mom and dad were beaming. Ann and Don called. I thought I was one step away from being an Olympian. Kim, Betty, and Hilary also qualified for Olympic Trials. As it turned out, all of Bela's girls made it to Baltimore and the Olympic Trials.

What I didn't know was that not everyone who qualified for Trials was going to compete there. And the whole Olympic selection process was going to become controversial.

By the way Bela was acting during training in Houston before we left for Trials, we could tell that he was feeling pressured and was fighting some sort of battle. It turned out that because of Betty's back injury and Shannon's elbow injury, there was a dispute brewing over how the Trials were going to work and how the final Olympic team was going to be selected.

Bela knew that Betty's back injury was serious enough to prevent her from competing at the Olympic Trials. Steve Nunno, Shannon's coach, had pulled her out of U.S. Championships after the compulsories because of her elbow. After much discussion among Bela, Steve, other coaches, and the federation, it was decided that Betty could be petitioned onto the team at some sort of training camp after Trials. Shannon was going to be allowed to compete at the Trials even though she did not finish U.S. Championships. And after Michelle Campi injured her elbow during last-minute preparations for Trials, the federation decided to let her U.S. Championships scores stand as her Trials scores, too. Michelle wasn't going to have to compete in Baltimore at all.

At that time, U.S. Championships was supposed to count 30 percent toward qualifying for the Olympic team and Trials was to count 70 percent. For Shannon, Trials would be 100 percent of her score. For Michelle, Championships would be 100 percent of her score.

This seemed weird: We were going to have Trials, but not really. None of us knew what was happening. Bela convinced us to just keep working and think only about Baltimore. It was a very tense time, especially for Bela.

Maybe because he was under pressure, Bela made a decision I will never forget. The gym, I could handle. It was just training, trying to get better. It's what I wanted and needed. Staying in Houston for Christmas was upsetting, but I understood that, too.

But our family had been planning a surprise birthday party for my father's fiftieth birthday. My mom and dad and the whole family was going to meet at Uncle Don's. We scheduled the party for a Sunday, when I knew I was going to have all afternoon and evening off. Sunshine and her mother even flew to Houston for the party, and everyone was looking forward to it.

Bela found out about the party and decided I couldn't go. He scheduled a late-afternoon practice, and Martha told me, "You don't need to be going to parties and eating all that cake. All you think about is parties."

I thought, "Yeah, right. Me, Kerri Strug, the outgoing cake-eating party girl."

I'll never forget that episode. My time with my family was so special to me that I got very upset when Bela infringed on it. Only after our workout the next day was I permitted to go with my family for a quick dinner at a Chinese restaurant for my dad's birthday. I'll never forget the fortune that I got in my cookie that night. It said: "Your life will be happy and peaceful." "Someday, maybe," I thought.

When we arrived in Baltimore, I wrote in my diary on June 9, 1992: "I have dreamed of this day since I was eight years old. I've dreamed of going to the Olympics, and now I have the chance. I've moved away from home, haven't had much of a social life, and have sacrificed so much. All to come down to this one meet. Crazy, huh?"

My whole family came in for Trials, including Lisa, who actually chose to be in Baltimore cheering for me instead of attending her own graduation ceremony from UCLA. I thought that was pretty incredible and unselfish of her.

Before Trials began, we were told that the seven qualifiers and Betty would go to France for a pre-Olympic training camp, where the final six-member competing team and an alternate would be determined. So I thought to myself, "Okay, just make it into the top seven and you'll be fine."

"I'm thrilled and scared," I wrote in my diary, moments before leaving the hotel for Baltimore Arena. "I've done these routines so many times. I know I should have more self-confidence. This should be a piece of cake. I know I can do these routines. I'll write to you again tonight. Hopefully, I'll have great news."

And sure enough, I did come back with great news. I was in third place after compulsories, behind Shannon, who was in first, and Kim, who was in second. Hilary was in trouble, however, standing in eighth place.

But even while the meet took place, there was more controversy brewing. Bela was going crazy over the inconsistent scoring, especially as it applied to Kim and Hilary. For some reason, once I began competing I was fine. I was confident and was getting good scores. But Kim was the world champion; she had just won U.S. Championships, and Bela thought she was not getting all the points she deserved.

Before optionals, I went for a massage, hoping to relax before the competition began. The trainer told me, "Whoa, Kerri, your muscles are so tight I need a hammer to loosen them up." My whole body was tied up in knots. Other gymnasts, coaches, and federation people felt the same way. There was so much tension all over the arena.

"Just make the top seven," I told myself as we marched in for introductions, "and worry about everything else later." It was the toughest mental test I had in my life to that point. And through three routines I could not have responded better. I hit vault, bars, and beam, and I hit them strongly. I even got a 9.95 on vault. One judge scored me with a perfect 10. I was competing at my best. But just as I was beginning to think I had made the team, I fell apart on the floor, which is usually automatic for me. I fell on my first pass, which had a new element that I'd added only weeks before Trials. Worst of all, I went out of bounds. The fall was a mandatory half-point deduction. Going out of bounds was a mandatory one-tenth deduction per foot. Since I went out with both feet, the best possible score I could get was a 9.3. I scored a 9.262 and was in total shock.

As I jogged off the floor, I was so upset and disappointed my whole body tingled. All those years. All the work. All the sacrifice.

The dreams. Everything seemed gone just like that. As I walked down the stairs from the floor, Martha stated the obvious. "You blew it," she told me.

I slumped into a chair and looked up into the stands, searching for my parents, Lisa, Kevin, and Sunshine. "Yup, I blew it," I thought to myself, trying to hold back my tears.

But lo and behold, I hadn't. When the competition was over and they posted the scores, I'd actually finished third overall. My compulsory and optional routines up until the floor were so strong, I actually had room to spare. If it hadn't been for the fall and the steps out of bounds, I could have finished higher.

I was thrilled, but Kim and Bela were very upset about the way things turned out for her. Kim made the team and actually should have been ranked number one, when you took into account how she did at U.S. Championships and Trials. But Shannon was ranked first based on her scores from Trials alone. Making matters worse was that Hilary missed making the team by less than two-tenths of a point. She was a little weak on bars because of a shoulder injury. She had always been a strong competitor, but her injury occurred at the worst possible time.

There was a great deal of confusion about whether we all really did make the team. After scores were tabulated at Trials, the seven top scorers lined up and the announcer introduced us to the crowd at Baltimore Arena. But even as we walked in behind the American flag, so proud to be on the team, we knew there was a chance that the team would change between Baltimore and Barcelona. We just didn't know which of us was going to be disappointed. "Ladies and gentlemen, your 1992 Olympic gymnastics team," the announcer said. "Shannon Miller, Kim Zmeskal, Kerri Strug, Dominique Dawes, Michelle Campi, Kim Kelly, and Wendy Bruce."

Michelle hadn't competed at Trials and no one knew if her injury would improve in time for Barcelona. But her scores from U.S. Championships were enough to place her in the top seven. Confusion still prevailed.

I watched Hilary leave the arena, with her head down and holding her father's hand. It was one of the saddest things I had ever seen. Just like that, Hilary's gymnastics career was over. I felt so bad for her. For the first time in my life, I saw Kim look less than 100 percent confident. Her second place affected her.

The federation told our coaches that there would be a pre-Olympic camp either in Tampa or Orlando, Florida, where the final Olympic team would be determined. Betty would be allowed to compete at the camp, and Michelle would be permitted to demonstrate that she had recovered from the elbow injury. It meant that for sure one of the seven girls introduced at Trials would be cut.

Coaches were going to watch the routines and then meet to determine the Olympic team. A lot of people believed that either Kim Kelly or Wendy Bruce would be cut. I read one story that predicted I would be cut, since I was only fourteen and could try again in 1996.

Bela assured me that my routines were too strong for that to happen. And my two heroes in the sport were in my corner. Mary Lou Retton said my Trials performance was so strong, she predicted an individual medal for me in Barcelona. "Nobody knew me before 1984, either," she told the press after Trials. "In some ways, the best thing you can have going for you is the element of surprise. That's what Kerri has going for her right now. I wouldn't be surprised if she did something big in Barcelona."

A few days later, Nadia Comaneci said, "The only difference between Kerri and Kim is a little power and a lot of experience.

Kerri is the closest to Kim that I have seen of anybody. Not even Shannon is as talented as Kerri. With a good competition, everything correct, Kerri could be a big surprise in Barcelona."

I wrote only one thing in my diary about finishing in the top seven at Trials. "I've accomplished my dream."

Injuries were my only concern as we prepared for the pre-Olympic camp, which was scheduled for Orlando on July 9. Since Bela never eased up on the workouts and my whole body was sore, I was a little worried. Even though we had gone through a grueling series of competitions and had just finished Trials, Bela still worked us out twice a day. Even when the electricity went out at the ranch a couple of days before leaving for Orlando and we thought we'd get a break, Bela just opened all the doors of the gym and we practiced anyway.

"I'm not a happy camper right now," I wrote in my diary on June 28. "My back is killing me. What worries me is it feels like it's the bone, not just the muscle. Both my legs are sore. It's always something, isn't it? Oh, well. Like they say: No pain, no Barcelona, Spain. . . . I don't see why we have to have another trial. Haven't we proven ourselves enough? Oh, please, let me remain on the team."

When we got to Brown's Gym in Orlando for the second Olympic Trials, all the coaches and Kathy Kelly, the federation's program director, sat on one side of the gym. The tryout was closed to the public and the media. Some of the coaches had pencils and notepads, as if they were judges. Others just watched. I was happy to see Kathy Kelly and Roe Kruetzer, a couple of great ladies in the USA Gymnastics organization. They have never had any agenda other than what's best for the athletes and the team.

Once again, there was a lot of pressure, but maybe because there were no television cameras or fans, everyone looked really good and relaxed. I could not believe how strong Michelle Campi performed. Betty looked good, too. Everyone got through compulsories and optionals without major breaks, except for Dominique Dawes and Kim Zmeskal, who each had one minor slipup.

The worst part about the whole second Olympic Trials was that we couldn't tell how we were doing. No scores were posted. We just did our routines, moving from apparatus to apparatus, and then went back to the hotel and waited. I sat in my room while all the coaches and USA Gymnastics officials met, praying that I would not get a telephone call informing me that I was off the team.

Then just as I was writing "I wonder who's going home tomorrow" in my diary, someone knocked on the door, scaring me. At the door was a trainer, who told me that Kim Kelly had been the one who was cut.

"P.S.," I wrote before going to bed. "I just found out that Kim Kelly was the unlucky one. That's really sad for her. It doesn't seem fair. But I guess that means I've really made the Olympic team. I've accomplished a dream. I'm going to Barcelona. Gotta go. I've got to call Mom and Dad with the great news."

6

"Did I make it? Did I make it?"

❁

I was proud to be an American. I arrived in Orlando, joining my gymnastics teammates and other U.S. Olympians as we prepared to leave for France, en route to Spain. I felt so warm and energized. Everywhere I went, I know I was bouncing along like it was Christmas morning.

Sure, I had big goals for Barcelona. Simply making the Olympic team was not going to be enough for me; I wanted more. But when I first pulled on the USA Olympic colors, I wasn't thinking about all that had brought me to this point. I was thinking only about how proud I was to be standing there with the best athletes in the world, representing my country and the sport I loved.

The seven of us who made that Olympic women's gymnastics team went through processing with the other athletes, got our credentials and our photo IDs, had our physicals, and were outfitted with all sorts of clothes and gifts. Sponsors gave us warmups, pins, official opening ceremony outfits, shirts, shoes, watches, hats, bags. We each got a USA leather jacket. We even got to adopt our own Cabbage Patch Kid. I chose a little blond doll named Ashley. I met swimmers Matt Biondi, Crissy Ahmann-Leighton, Janet Evans, and lots of other athletes from different sports.

It was a wild, hectic, but wonderful day. And when we were finally processed, we still had more places to go and things to do. We went back to the hotel, where we had our first national-team press conference.

But the mood of the press conference brought us all down. Almost every question was about Kim Kelly. Understandably, Kim and her family were not happy about her being cut from the team. People were talking about lawsuits, the politics in the sport, the unfairness of the whole ordeal. I tried to stay away from the controversy as much as I could. But everyone in the world seemed to have an opinion concerning whether Kim Kelly should have been on the team and how the selection process should have been handled.

I knew we had seven talented girls going to France for the pre-Olympic training camp, although I did wish Hilary could have been with us somehow. In France, coaches were going to decide which six girls would compete in Barcelona and who would be the alternate. Although we wound up with a good team, I did think that what happened to Kim Kelly was unfair. I couldn't imagine how bad I would have felt had I been the one cut after being told I had made it.

I was relieved when the only questions for me at the press conference were about making the team and the upcoming competition. I also got a question about being the youngest American on the 1992 Olympic Team. I didn't realize it at the time, but by qualifying for the Games at fourteen I was probably going to be the youngest American Olympian in a long, long time. International gymnastics rules in 1992 required Olympic athletes to be at least fifteen by the end of the Olympic calendar year. Since I was going to be fifteen in late November, I barely made the cut. After 1996, the rule changed again.

The minimum age for Olympic gymnasts was raised to sixteen.

"Being fourteen isn't something I think about a lot," I said in response to the question. "I never think of my age as a factor. I have already experienced a lot in this sport."

Finally, I was asked about my plans after Barcelona. "One thing about being fourteen, I just don't think I'm going to have gymnastics out of my system when these games are over," I replied. "I'm not talking about Atlanta and 1996, but I enjoy gymnastics a lot right now. I know that everything I've done, all the hard work, has been worth it, and I want to keep going."

As difficult as the road had been for me to that point in my career and as much as I'd had to overcome, I wanted to keep traveling down that road after Barcelona, whether it led to another World Championship team, a collegiate career, or a second Olympic Games. I did consider making that 1992 Olympic team a once-in-a-lifetime opportunity, the highest point I ever would reach in gymnastics. But somehow I knew I wasn't done with the sport.

International gymnastics fans and judges favored young, tiny, acrobatic girls at the time. In 1992, I was. Small and slender. Our entire team was tiny, and nearly all of the teams considered contenders for the medals had small, acrobatic girls. Shannon was 4 feet 6. I was 4 feet 8. The only American girls taller than 4 feet 9 were Wendy Bruce, who was 5 feet 1, and Betty, who was 5 feet 3. I figured that four years from this point, I would be eighteen, maybe a little bigger, maybe not so limber, and perhaps not the kind of girl who could make a U.S. Olympic team. I didn't know if I could handle four more years of intense training like the year and a half I had just survived at Bela's. And the last thing I wanted was to be away from home again for so long.

After Barcelona, I planned to just keep doing gymnastics at

whatever level I happened to be. I made a list of what I wanted to accomplish after the Olympics. Two items on the list were "Finish high school. Get a gymnastics scholarship."

Sunshine and I always talked about going to UCLA and competing together. Some elite gymnasts didn't have college gymnastics in their plans. They figured that after they had reached the sport's highest level, NCAA gymnastics was not for them. I understood how those athletes felt, but for me, gymnastics is gymnastics, and any gymnastics is good.

Many elites couldn't compete in college even if they wanted to because they were professionals. Athletes like Shannon, Betty, and Kim lost their collegiate eligibility by taking federation, tour, and prize money. I still hadn't done that.

Bela and others have always told me that I should have capitalized on reaching the elite level and turned professional. I was told that even though I couldn't compete in college gymnastics if I turned pro, I had other possibilities. Some of Bela's elites had gone on to become college cheerleaders. Hilary was talking about using her gymnastics background to get into competitive diving.

"There's good money out there for you," Bela told me.

But I have never looked at gymnastics as a means to an end. I have never looked at the Olympic Games as anything other than a privilege and an honor. The federation had plans for a post-Olympic gymnastics tour in 1992, and I planned to participate. But I still chose not to be paid for it. And me, a cheerleader? I don't think so. I wasn't a diver, either. After Barcelona, I just wanted to keep competing in the sport I loved. I was going to the Games with high hopes, but no feeling of pressure. I really liked that situation.

For Kim, things were different, although she loved gymnastics no less than I did. Kim was devoted to the sport. But Kim's whole life had been pointed toward Barcelona, whether by her choice or not. Because of all her successes and the attention she had received, Barcelona would be Kim's great stage and probably the defining time of her career. And she was going to have the biggest audience possible: the entire world.

Kim got most of the questions at the pre-games press conference, questions on every subject imaginable. What did she think of Barcelona? What commercial opportunities had she had? Had she thought about competing in front of a television audience of more than a billion people? Had the pressure and attention been too much?

Kim was doing all sorts of TV, radio, and newspaper interviews. Earlier, NBC got her to do some promos and interviews. Then after the formal press conference, newspaper reporters from all over the world surrounded Kim again and backed her into a corner. The reporters squeezed tighter and tighter around Kim, pushing their microphones into her face and trying to get closer to her. Kim didn't say too much about it at the time, but the burden of those Games was great on her. You could see it in her face. I think by the end of that day in Orlando, we were all just ready for the Olympic Games to begin.

And the next morning, we were on our way. We boarded a 747 headed for France and had a whole nine hours to rest and relax before we arrived. Bela and Martha kept reminding us not to get too caught up in the atmosphere. They emphasized why we were going to the Olympic Games: to compete.

The seven of us sat together on the plane and began thinking about what lay ahead of us. I popped a piece of bubble gum into my mouth and opened my diary. "I'm on a charter flight along with all of the other athletes going to France," I wrote. "Let me tell you what it's like to be an Olympian."

And I wrote for hours, talking about how proud I was to be on that team. I listed all the neat things that had happened to me since I became an Olympian. I ended the entry with "but there's still so much left to do. I can't wait for the competition to begin." I pushed my seat back and slept peacefully the rest of the way.

Good thing, too. Once we got to France, we were caught up in a frantic series of last-minute preparations for the Games. We worked out hard twice a day. Not only were we all trying to make the six-member competing team for the Games, but we were also trying to convince Bela and the other coaches that we deserved a good place in the team's lineup.

Placement in a team lineup is always important in a competition, both for the team and for the individual. The first athletes up in a competition rarely get scored as high as they would if they were the fifth or sixth athlete in their team's lineup. Judges like to leave room for improvement on their scorecards. So coaches tend to put solid, consistent athletes first on an apparatus, with the hope that the scores can start at a good level and build higher. Hilary always competed first on U.S. teams, giving us a good starting point. But Hilary wasn't in Barcelona. Who was going to be the starter? Bela and the coaches had to find just the right people to lead us off.

After the starter on an apparatus, girls who are weaker in a particular event then usually compete second or third in the rotation, in the hopes that they can ride the momentum provided by the first girl. The strongest athletes usually go fourth, fifth, and sixth. If everything goes as planned, the team will do great. If the first girl is strong and every girl builds the score higher from that point, the fifth and sixth competitors stand a chance of earning high 9.9s or even a 10. This is a great strategy for the team and benefits the girls individually, since the top thirty-six athletes in the team competition move on to individual all-arounds. Most often, the athletes who qualify for individual all-arounds are the ones who go fourth, fifth, or sixth in their team's rotation. These are usually the stronger girls, sure, but they also receive a slight edge from judges because of where they are in the lineup. Every tenth of even hundredth of a point counts.

Since I was reigning vault champion and was strong on the floor, I felt my chances of being fourth or fifth in the rotation on those events were pretty good. On beam and bars, I had worked hard and was much more consistent than when I first arrived at Bela's. But all I could do was hope for the best in those events, even though I knew I probably wouldn't get the best positions.

As we trained in France the last few days before the Games, it became obvious that Michelle Campi was injured. Her elbow was better, but she had hamstring and hip injuries that limited her. Dominique Dawes was also suffering with a neck injury. Wendy had a few aches, too. I was sore, Kim was sore, and Betty's back still bothered her. Shannon's elbow also still hurt her, but she looked good. Obviously, none of us was exactly 100 percent.

Along with the aches and pains, we were still trying to become the strong, unified force that we had been at the World Championships just one year earlier. We had spent so much time competing against each other to get to Barcelona that we couldn't just flip a switch and suddenly be the close-knit team we had been at Worlds. We had been to meets everywhere, had competed within our own gyms, and had gone to nationals, Trials, and the second trial in Orlando. We were sore everywhere. People expected us to pull together like sisters, but we found that hard.

We did like each other; we were just having a hard time realizing that we no longer were competing against each other and we needed to come together as a team.

By the time we checked into the athletes' village a few days before the opening ceremonies, we had begun to open up a little more. We talked more often, worked well together, and felt more comfortable.

The village was a twenty-minute bus ride from the Olympic center in Barcelona. It was located on the Mediterranean shore, with really nice views. We had comfortable apartments, although the rooms weren't air-conditioned and Spain was *very* hot, as bad as Houston.

After we got settled into our rooms at the Olympic village, something great happened. Maybe the coaches knew we still needed to jell as a team or we just needed a break. The day before the opening ceremonies the coaches cut short our afternoon workout and encouraged us all to go for a walk together. We were going to see a few sights and maybe call our parents.

That walk turned out to be one of the highlights of the trip for all of us. In a way, it also brought us closer together. The USA Dream Team—the original Dream Team, with Michael Jordan, Larry Bird, Magic Johnson, and Charles Barkley—pulled up in their team bus just as we were walking by the athletes' accreditation area. I'm a *huge* basketball fan. I've cheered for my favorite teams—the Arizona Wildcats, the UCLA Bruins, the Duke Blue Devils, the Phoenix Suns, and the Houston Rockets—all my life. When I saw the Dream Team, I was ecstatic.

"It's the Dream Team, it's the Dream Team!" I shouted. I thought it was the neatest thing. And fortunately, or so I thought, I'd brought with me a new camera that my mom got me for the Olympics. I just freaked out, standing there, trying to catch a glimpse of the players. I was taking pictures of everything, even the bus. I didn't care. It was the Dream Team's bus! Later I realized that I had loaded my new camera incorrectly. Not a single picture I took that day came out.

Still, the whole scene was unforgettable. Larry Bird noticed the commotion we were making outside the bus and invited us in to meet the team. He didn't have to tell me twice! We sprinted onto the bus. The guys were all so nice. Larry Bird was great, posing with all of us, giving us pins. David Robinson seemed sincerely happy to see us. Magic Johnson was incredibly friendly. He just smiled, asked a lot of questions, and wished us good luck. Charles Barkley was hilarious.

I spoke with all of them. That was one time in my life that I definitely was not shy. What a fantastic experience! I just wish I had the pictures to prove it. And I thought meeting the Dream Team brought us together as a team. It was an experience we shared. If the Dream Team players could put aside their rivalries and millions of dollars for their country, we could also form a team.

"Now, missing the opening ceremonies won't be so bad," I wrote in my diary that night. Before that day, I had been a little upset that after all the training and sacrifices I had made, I wasn't going to get to march with the Americans at the Olympic opening ceremonies. The gymnastics competition was scheduled to begin the morning after the ceremonies, so the coaches decided we needed to get to bed early and rest. On July 26 we had an afternoon workout, ate a light dinner, and then watched some of the opening ceremonies on TV. That night I slept poorly.

On the bus ride into Barcelona the next day, we saw all the sights and felt the electricity; I got all fired up and ready to compete. Barcelona seemed to be alive with people and bright colors. The Olympic venues were spectacular. We saw people from all over the world walking around clutching their Olympic tickets or sitting at sidewalk cafés enjoying the atmosphere.

The gymnastics competition was held at the Palau Sant Jordi, a new arena near Olympic Stadium at the top of Montjuic. When

I reached the arena, I just stared at it in awe for a second and then told Betty, "Well, there it is. Our dream house."

For Shannon, our dream house became her palace, the place where she would become the new queen of the sport. She was on her way to an unforgettable experience, a five-medal bonanza. The Palau Sant Jordi was the place where we as a team would earn the best Olympic finish ever in a nonboycotted Games. But for Kim and me, our dream house was a house of cards.

The house first tumbled down on Kim. She had been so perfect in so many big meets for so long. She had been the best in the world.

All my life, from the first time I heard about her when I was a junior, the word "clutch" was always mentioned when describing Kim. Like everyone else in the world, I expected Kim to save her most sensational performance for the biggest meet of her life.

Maybe those expectations were too great. Maybe all the build-up to that one moment caused the slightest crack in Kim's usually strong-as-steel concentration. Or maybe it was just a fluke.

But on her first routine in Barcelona, on a simple cartwheel and back handspring flip-flop that she had done perfectly thousands of times before, Kim slipped and fell to the mats, a mandatory five-tenths deduction. Less than a minute into the Olympic competition that the entire world thought would belong to her, Kim was on the floor. The shocked look on her face when she climbed back onto the beam said it all. She scored a 9.350. I've never heard 16,000 people sit so quietly. Everyone knew it was going to be next to impossible for Kim to make up so much ground and make it to individual all-arounds.

Somehow Kim managed to make it through the rest of the compulsories pretty clean. As for the rest of us, we were doing fine. Dominique and Wendy competed earlier in the day—they were our starters—and did very well. Because of her injuries, Michelle Campi wound up being the alternate, so she had to watch. Shannon was near perfect. Betty was great. And I could not have been happier, scoring nothing but 9.8s and 9.9s during the compulsories. We were in second place overall, behind the Unified Team, which was the name given to the former Soviet countries at those 1992 Games.

After we were done for the day, Kim still looked shaken. Bela and Martha weren't too thrilled, either. As we all walked into the press area afterward, I saw Bela and Martha talking quietly, shaking their heads. It was as if there had been a death in the family.

"I just got into a hurry," Kim told the press afterward. "I don't really remember ever falling on something like that before. I just hurried it too much. I think maybe I can still make it to all-arounds if I hit everything the rest of the way."

None of us said very much to Kim, other than to offer her encouragement. What could we possibly have said? Everyone knew she would have a hard time making it to all-arounds. And besides, we had to focus on winning a team medal. We not only had a lot of ground to catch up on if we were going to battle the Unified Team for the gold, but Romania and China were close on our heels in the race for the silver and bronze. If we didn't hit our optional routines two days from now, we stood a chance of not winning a medal at all.

Individually, Shannon was in first place overall after compulsories, just ahead of the Unified Team's Svetlana Boguinskaia, Ukraine's Tatiana Gutsu, and Hungary's Henrietta Onodi. Betty was in good shape in eighth place after the first day. I was in thirteenth, with a good shot at making it to all-arounds—my dream. Kim was in thirty-second.

"You'll never believe what happened today, there were some pretty shocking results," I wrote in my diary back at the village.

"I did real well. On floor, I did the routine of my life. Vault went great. Everything else was fine. Now, for the unbelievable news—Kim is in thirty-second place. She fell on beam. She's only two-tenths of a point behind me. The U.S. still is in second, barely. I sure hope we can pull it off. And oh, please, let me make all-around finals."

I knew my all-around hopes depended not just on hitting my routines, but on the optionals lineup. In optionals, we were going to compete together as a team, all six of us one after the other on each apparatus. During compulsories, we competed separately. Dominique and Wendy competed in the morning, then Betty and I were on one apparatus in the early afternoon, while Kim and Shannon were on another in the late afternoon. But on the deciding day of the competition, the top four teams after compulsories always performed together, head-to-head. The teams rotated from apparatus to apparatus so the fans could see how the competition was going event by event. This system always made team optionals very tension-filled and dramatic.

Bela waited until the evening before optionals to tell us what the lineup would be. He put me third on everything but vault, where I was going to be fourth. I was disappointed. Being national champion on vault and performing so well on the floor during compulsories, I thought I would be at least fourth on floor and fifth on vault. Since Kim was the world champion, I knew Bela would have her going sixth on most events. But I was hoping I would receive a better position in the lineup.

I knew I was going to have to hold my own and earn every hundredth of a point that I received. I still hadn't seen my parents and was feeling lonely. "It's up to me," I wrote on the morning of team optionals. "I am going to hit everything. I have to do it. I can do it and I will do it."

I kept trying to think positive. By the time we began warmups, I came to the conclusion that it was too late to do a thing. I kept telling myself to concentrate on the routines, only the routines. Just hit. I went through each routine in my mind and had a great warmup. I felt nervous but confident. I looked up into the stands and found my parents, Kevin, and Lisa. But I did feel better when my father gave me a thumbs-up sign. I nodded to him and was ready to compete.

I told myself, "You can and you will."

We started out on bars. And it was like magic. I'd had competitions before in which I hit every routine, but never in my life had I done so well in a big competition. And this was the biggest of all. I hit everything cleanly and confidently. I felt as if it wasn't the Olympics at all, just another day at Bela's gym or another verification; only this time I was proving myself in front of the entire world, not just the summer campers. Shaky? Not even. I hit everything. Bars was a 9.862. Beam was a 9.75 despite a subpar landing. I really wasn't paying much attention to what anyone else was doing because I was so focused on my routines. The only other American I noticed on bars was Kim, who nailed her routine. We went to floor and I hit again—a 9.837. It was almost perfect. And vault was even closer to perfect—a 9.95!

When my feet stuck into the mat after vault, I heard the crowd screaming and applauding and I felt a chill go up my spine. I couldn't help but laugh. Bela gave me a huge hug when I bounced down the stairs into his arms. Martha was saying, "Great, great." As a team, we had lost a little ground to Romania along the way, but only because the Romanians hit everything strong. The Unified Team had the gold won and the Romanians were barely ahead of us for the silver, but my vault helped lock up the bronze for the USA. Shannon and Betty kept up their strong performances and Kim was hitting everything, too, although I wasn't paying much attention to Kim's scores. I was sure that I'd reached my ultimate goal. I was sure I'd made individual all-arounds.

But when I finally looked up at the scoreboard after my vault, I couldn't find my name. They hadn't posted any individual scores. Then I saw Kim nail her vault, scoring a 9.95, and Bela and Martha were going crazy. Bela let out a big yell and shook his fists into the air. He lifted Kim into the air and I heard him telling her, "You did it, you did it. Kim, you made it."

I thought to myself, "What?" I was in a panic as I gathered my things and began marching off the floor to prepare for the awards ceremony. I heard someone else telling Kim, "You made it, you made it." I looked at the scoreboard again and couldn't tell anything about individual all-arounds.

I found my family in the stands. "Did I make it? Did I make it?" I shouted.

Lisa ran down the stairs toward me, yelling "That's my sister, that's my sister!" at the security guards who were trying to stop her. Good thing Lisa is fluent in Spanish or who knows what those guards would have done.

I shouted at her again: "Did I make it?" I was petrified.

Lisa shook her head. No.

When I saw Bela lift Kim into the air after her vault, I knew my dream of making all-arounds was gone. But I didn't want to believe it. When Lisa told me, it hit me really hard. I stood paralyzed. Tears filled my eyes and I had such an empty feeling inside my stomach. I had just given one of the best performances of my life in a big competition—and it was not enough. I easily ranked among the top thirty-six gymnasts in the world. But that wasn't enough, either, because three other Americans were ahead of me, and only three girls per country could advance to all-arounds.

I hadn't really paid attention to Kim most of the night. But while I was concentrating on my routines, Kim put together the most spectacular performance of her career and made up all the ground on me. She outscored me by .014 of a point. Just .014 of a point. After all the sacrifices and dreams, I fell short by .014 of a point. My whole body was shaking.

I walked up to Shannon, Betty, and Kim as we were standing in the staging area waiting for the medal ceremony to begin. I told them, "Great job, guys. Do great at all-arounds." Honestly, I don't remember what else happened. I was in shock. We marched into the arena, got our medals, received flowers, and listened to the Olympic anthem, which was played for the Unified Team. I hardly remember any of it. I had a stunned look on my face the whole time. All I could think about was that .014 of a point.

What could I have done better? Would a better spot in the lineup have made the difference? Why did I have to hop on my beam dismount? Why had I not quite reached my goals? Once again I had fallen into the shadows, just short of my dream.

I walked into the press area and went straight to the back of the room. I covered my face with my hands and burst into tears. I couldn't stop crying. I was hardly able to breathe. I sat there for almost an hour as Kim, Shannon, and Betty sat under the bright lights at the front of the room answering questions. "Just a little more and you would have made all-arounds," I finally whispered to myself. "Just a little more."

Someone asked Bela about my great performance barely falling short. "Kerri made no mistakes," he said. "She was one of the biggest reasons why we got the team bronze medal, but probably no one will remember. It's sad. She was great, but yes, it was so sad to think that she missed the all-arounds. Kerri did nothing to be ashamed about."

Then why did I feel so ashamed? I finally got to see my family late that night. I sank into their arms. They told me they loved me and that I did great. "You're just fourteen," Lisa said. "You've accomplished so much."

I joined the rest of the team on the bus and rode back to the village. I got to my room and opened my diary. "This was a night I'll remember," I wrote. "Kim beat me by .014 to qualify for all-around finals. It's really weird. I got an Olympic medal and I'm miserable. This is the most upset and disappointed I've ever been.

"I'm so confused and discouraged. I know Kim deserved to make all-arounds. She earned it. But I thought I did, too. I'm not sure about everything. I'm really tired of always almost being there. Maybe I should just go home, go to school, and just do gym like I did before. Maybe I should just do it for fun."

Tatiana Gutsu of Ukraine wound up winning the all-around gold. Shannon took the silver, on the way to her five medals in those Games. Kim did not perform as strong as she did in team optionals and stepped out of bounds on the floor. She finished tenth in all-arounds. Betty didn't score as well as we all hoped and wound up twelfth. And strangest of all, Bela and Martha announced their retirements before the meet even was over.

No one thing led to their decision, but many things combined: the politics, the Trials, all the pressure heaped on Kim, the long hours they were spending in the gym, their many years in the sport. And after the thrill we all felt at World Championships in 1991, I think the Olympics were kind of a letdown for Bela and Martha.

They definitely were for me. I had a lot of thinking to do. Bela was gone, my Olympic dream vanished by .014 of a point, and I had no idea if I ever wanted to compete at that level again.

I never even got to say good-bye to Bela and Martha. After the final gymnastics events, they got on a plane the next morning. Just like that, after everything we had been through together, they were gone. I thought a lot about what I wanted to do with my gymnastics career. One minute I was convinced I wanted to make it to Atlanta in 1996. I felt more determined than ever to commit everything I had toward reaching my dream of making it to the all-arounds. I felt I would put up with anything and everything if I could just reach that dream. But the next minute I was depressed and discouraged, not sure how much I had left in me.

I decided that since my family was going to vacation in Europe after the Games, I would just try to sort everything out when we got back to Tucson. "I can't dwell on it now," I wrote in my diary. "I got to the Olympics and I got a medal. That's a lot more than most people ever achieve. But right now I think I want to continue so I can show everyone how good Kerri Strug really is."

We skipped the closing ceremonies, and our first stop on our vacation was Euro-Disney. One day at the park, I popped a piece of Bazooka Joe into my mouth and read the wrapper. "Nobody does it better than you," it said.

7

"I just sort of fell into a shell"

❦

We have something called the twenty-four-hour rule in our family. It has come in handy on several occasions, helping us think things through whenever one of us is making an important decision. My dad came up with the twenty-four-hour rule mostly because of me.

A lot of times when I was homesick or tired of the hard training at Bela's before 1992, I'd call Mom and Dad, telling them I was ready to quit or ready to move to another gym. They always listened patiently and encouraged me, and I usually felt better about things after talking with them. But the incident that led to the establishment of the twenty-four-hour rule was when I hurt my hand so badly in practice before the 1991 World Trials. I called home and told Mom my hand was broken. I was devastated, because I thought the injury was going to ruin my chances of making the World Championship team. I told Mom on the phone, "What am I going to do? Why is this happening? I need you, Mom. I need you here."

After we hung up, Mom booked a flight to Houston the next morning. By that next day my hand was feeling better and I was in the gym doing some conditioning. Mom showed up at the gym expecting to see my hand in a cast and in need of some emotional support. I was surprised to see her and asked, "Why are you here?"

"I thought you broke your hand," she said.

"No, I don't think so. I'm just going to go get some X-rays and treatment. I think I'm fine," I said. And that was the genesis of the twenty-four-hour rule. I had a great visit with Mom and I did ultimately get some treatment for my hand, but it wasn't broken.

Dad wasn't thrilled about paying all that money for a plane ticket when all I really needed was a day to get myself together. Ever since then, unless it's an emergency, whenever any of us has had to make a big decision in our lives we have always waited an extra twenty-four hours to think it through. Only after the twenty-four hours do we follow through with our decision.

While we were on vacation, I tried not to think about what I wanted to do with my gymnastics career. I just wanted to have some fun, but I couldn't help but think about my broken dreams. While we were together in Europe, I changed my mind again and again about what I wanted to do. One day I'd decide to focus on gymnastics and on getting to the all-arounds at the 1996 Games. But twenty-four hours later, I'd think to myself, "I'll just move on to something else." Twenty-four hours after that, I would change my mind again.

I was on an airplane back to Tucson when I wrote in my diary: "I still haven't made up my mind. I have no clue about what I should do. My first fourteen years were planned toward the '92 Olympics. Now I've got to decide about the rest of my life. I'm sure whatever I do I'll be happy because I've got a wonderful family that will do whatever it can to help me. But I need to make a decision."

I spent several days in Tucson visiting friends and trying to relax, but I was restless the whole time. I finally realized I was restless because, as I told people before the Olympics, gymnastics was still not out of my system. I couldn't leave it behind or shake the disappointment of coming so close to fulfilling all my dreams.

I watched some tapes of the Olympic competition and the results never got any easier to accept. If anything, I felt worse every time I saw how strong I competed, only to fall short. Some people thought that because I experienced so much heartbreak in Barcelona I would turn away from the sport. But what happened only made me want it more. I was proud to be an Olympic team member and a medal winner, but I still felt empty inside.

There was no real end to Barcelona, no closure. Bela and Martha left before I could say good-bye, and that .014 of a point made it seem like the competition wasn't over. And for me, I guess it wasn't.

I decided that I wanted Atlanta. Nothing and no one was going to keep me from reaching my dream.

I waited the prescribed twenty-four hours, and after it felt as determined as ever. I spent a few more days with my family and friends, and my decision was the same. Competing in 1996 was what I wanted. I talked about it with Mom, Dad, Lisa, and Kevin and they could all see the determination in my eyes. Kevin even told me one day that he knew I was too competitive to let what happened in Barcelona be the last accomplishment of my career.

Dad said he would call Bela and talk about where I might want to continue my career. After all, another four years training and living away from home was a long time. Dad knew the triangle had to be perfect for me, or I could be in for trouble. I wasn't crazy about being away from my family for so long again. In fact, all along this was the sticking point in my decision. I had spent more than one and a half years at Bela's before Barcelona, the hardest time of my life. Could I possibly stand four more years away from home? I had no idea.

But I knew I couldn't walk away from the competition. After Bela talked with Dad, we made a list of several gyms that would help me continue improving and competing at a high level. We decided to look into some possibilities for host families and get to know the coaches during the post-Olympic gymnastics tour.

The 1992 tour had nine stops, and all the best coaches took part in it. I got a chance to be around people like Steve Nunno and Peggy Liddick, Kevin and Rita Brown, Kelli Hill, and all the other coaches from the gyms we were considering. Bela was at a few of the tour stops, too, but we realized that he was sincere about his retirement. I spoke with Bela about the pros and cons of certain gyms, and he helped me decide. The tour was fun—no pressure and great crowds at every stop. I finally narrowed my possibilities down to three gyms: Geza Pozsar's gym in Sacramento, Steve Nunno's in Oklahoma City, and Rita and Kevin Brown's in Orlando.

But the coach and the gym were just one part of the equation. My parents refused to compromise the triangle. The host family and the school *had* to be good and supportive.

At the end of the tour, with the school year about to start, we visited the gyms we were considering. At first I wanted to go to Nunno's, but people suggested that after competing in the shadows of Kim and Betty for so long at Bela's, I might not find Nunno's, where Shannon was coming off a five-medal performance, such a good idea. Personally, I didn't care. I liked competing with the best.

But we finally decided on Brown's Gymnastics in Orlando, which was the gym where we'd had the second Olympic trial.

Rita and Kevin Brown were great coaches with Olympic and World Championship experience. The school was great, too, but the clincher was the host family.

After Mom met Patty and Tom Exum and got to know them, she knew I wouldn't find a better family to live with. And once I got to know them, I realized Patty and Tom Exum truly were exceptional people. They reminded me of my parents. Patty was a teacher at Lake Highland, which was the school I attended. They both were outgoing and involved in the sport, and they treated me like their own child. Mrs. Exum often stayed up until 2:00 A.M. helping me with my homework or typing my school papers. I would tease her, telling her I didn't think my own mom would do that much for me. They have a daughter, Kelli, who is a gymnast about six years younger than I, and we became like sisters. They also have a son, Andy, who is a year younger than I, and we became great friends, too. It was the closest thing to having Mom, Dad, Kevin, and Lisa with me. I felt so lucky to have two families.

Honestly, the Exums were the biggest reason I went to Florida, and I remain good friends with them today. So once I began training at Brown's, everything seemed to be going along great. I was learning in the gym, making straight As in school, and living happily with the Exums. I thought, "These four years are going to fly by and I'll have those medals around my neck in no time."

Unfortunately, Rita and Kevin were having marital problems. Shortly after I had arrived, Kevin began spending less and less time in the gym until soon he was almost never there, but I didn't know why. I told Mom on the telephone one day, "I moved three thousand miles to train with Kevin Brown and he isn't really coaching me!"

We realized I needed a change, but since school was always such a big part of the equation, my parents said I needed to stay at Brown's until the end of the school semester, which was Christmas break. During the holidays, I went to Oklahoma City to train at Nunno's and decided to relocate there. Mom wasn't sure I would enjoy living in Shannon's shadow, but when I told her I wanted to give Steve's a try, she flew to Orlando, gathered all my things, and brought them to me in Oklahoma City. Just like that, I had another gymnastics home.

The decision to move to Steve's was abrupt, but Mom and Dad knew him pretty well from the time Lisa trained there. Lisa helped me make up my mind about going to Oklahoma City, too, because she said the school there, Heritage Hall, was terrific.

And Lisa was right: I loved it at Heritage Hall. It was the first school I attended since becoming an elite gymnast where I felt like just another student. Sure, I liked Northland Christian when I was at Bela's and I was glad the school was so accommodating to Bela's girls. But around Northland Christian, the gymnasts were always set apart from the rest of the student body. Gymnasts were allowed to wear sweats to school and to eat and even have classes apart from the regular students. It made you feel like an outsider.

At Heritage Hall, they understood that I had a gymnastics career, but the teachers and students still treated me like a regular student. One of the counselors there, Colonel Charles Stephenson, was really understanding and helped me feel like part of the school, not an outsider. I was just Kerri, not Kerri the Gymnast.

At Heritage Hall I became more social and started to overcome my shyness. Every day I got up early and went to morning workout, just like I did at Bela's and Brown's. But then I dressed in normal teenager clothes and went to school. It was important to me to dress and look like all the other girls in school. I became involved in normal school activities—class projects and clubs. And all my friends were nongymnasts. Rachel Hutto became my best friend at Heritage Hall, probably never realizing how much I appreciated her treating me like just another friend. I also became great friends with Holly Mankin. Whenever I went to a competition out of town, Rachel and Holly never made a big deal about the gymnastics part of it. They would just say, "Well, do good. When will you be back so we can go to the mall?" Rachel, Holly, and I *never* talked gymnastics, and that was a relief. Heritage Hall was also an open campus, so Rachel and I always went out for lunch. We went to her house or to the mall food court or to a bagel place that we both loved.

This was a very important time for me. My first few weeks in Oklahoma City went well. Steve had a great reputation as a coach and the school was working out, so two-thirds of the triangle seemed great. The only thing my family and I wondered about was the host family. Steve arranged for me to stay with the Garretts, a non-gymnastics family. Cherie Garrett and I had a class together at Heritage Hall and became friends, and I liked the Garretts.

Because the Garretts didn't really know the regimen of an elite gymnast, their schedules and mine were completely different. I ate, studied, and slept at different times than they did. It wasn't a bad environment at all, just different. Mrs. Garrett would make tempting homemade chocolate chip cookies, but I had to resist them because of the strict gymnastics regimen. They would take weekend trips and invite me along, not understanding why I couldn't go.

Training with Steve and Peggy was much different than I thought it would be, too. Since Steve used to coach for Bela,

I expected the same sort of training environment. But unlike Bela's, Steve's workouts were based on conditioning and a lot of repetition.

Training with Shannon was also different than what I had experienced with Kim, Betty, and Hilary. Shannon and I had gotten to know each other over the years through competitions, but we had never had a chance to become too close. At Steve's, we were together every day. We didn't exactly become best friends, because Shannon lived with her family in Edmond and we went to different schools. But once I began training with Shannon I realized that we could relate to each other because we had similar lifestyles.

From the day I first began training with Shannon at Steve's, I thought being around her would provide just the right motivation for me. Shannon pushed me a lot, but I think I pushed her, too. Just as when I was at Bela's, I never missed a workout. I taped up the injuries, took some Advil or Tylenol whenever my body ached, and just kept going.

And Steve and I both had much to prove to a lot of people. It was an interesting relationship.

Of course I hadn't forgotten Barcelona and knew that I never would. By training with Shannon every day, I could see where I stood in comparison with the very best. I know I shouldn't have been comparing myself with someone else, but I always did. I knew that facing Shannon would make me better. And in the first two meets in which we competed together for Steve's Dynamo Gymnastics team, I more than held my own. I beat Shannon in the preliminary round at the American Cup and beat her outright at the Dynamo Classic.

I think Steve wanted to prove that he could coach a top elite gymnast other than Shannon. I think he wanted to prove that he had had a lot to do with Shannon's success, not the other way around.

Steve was tough on me, pushing me hard every day, but I didn't mind at all. He wanted me to become his second world champion, and that was fine with me. I was learning a lot of new tricks and routines.

We put some difficult tumbling passes in my floor routine and I was hitting it all the time. I was doing great. We went to the World Trials in Salt Lake City and I won the competition outright.

By the spring of 1993, Shannon and I were on our way to Birmingham, England. It was my third World Championship team in a row. One year after Barcelona, I felt ready to make it to individual all-arounds and I thought I had the routines to get me there.

When we got to England, my floor routine was being called the toughest in the world. I was doing double layouts and whip-back combinations, which are full back somersaults without the gymnast's hands touching the floor.

Unfortunately, the World Championship judges did not give me credit for some of the tricks in my routine. I didn't have the necessary bonus points in my dance and jump combinations and it cost me dearly. Because the international scoring code had changed since 1992, judges gave bonus points on only those combinations that the International Gymnastics Federation included in their 1993 scoring code. In other words, even though I did more tricks, and more difficult tumbling tricks, than the other gymnasts, I didn't earn bonus points for them because I did not have the dance and jump combinations that were part of the new scoring code. When I hit my floor routine perfectly in the competition, it didn't matter to the judges. They had to follow the scoring code.

The top thirty-six athletes after the team competition qualified into the all-around finals, but only two gymnasts per country were allowed. Shannon qualified first, Dominique Dawes was
third. I finished fifth in the world, less than a tenth of a point
behind Dominique, but I could not compete in the all-arounds.

"Why has this happened to me again?" I cried to Mom on the
telephone after all-arounds. "Why does this always happen?"

After the changes in the code hurt me on the individual floor
routine finals, too, *International Gymnast* magazine praised my
World Championship routines and said that "anyone familiar
with the sport knows Strug was the top tumbler there."

I really was down. I wondered if I was cursed. I really thought
1993 was going to be my year, but it sure felt a lot like 1992. That
one competition and my disappointment changed everything
about my stay at Oklahoma City and Steve's.

Steve was upset about the scoring code mistake, too. He knew
I had proved myself on the floor but didn't get the scores. I
think Steve realized we should have paid more attention to the
scoring code. The good news for Steve was that Shannon won
the all-around championship. Once again I was training with the
world champion.

When we got on the flight back to the United States, Steve
sat next to me and tried to encourage me. "Look how much
you've grown as a gymnast," he said. "You've come a long way."

He pulled out a calendar and began going over the plan he had
for me in the coming months. He told me about the new tricks
he hoped I would learn, tricks that made better use of the scoring code. He assured me that he and Peggy would study the new
code and make sure I had enough bonus points on all my events.
We went over the upcoming schedule of meets and what I could
accomplish in them. He told me to keep working hard.

And when we got back to Oklahoma City, I began learning new tricks and new combination skills so I could work the code better. Steve and I were both looking for any little edge that could make the difference in a big competition. After I got over my disappointment, I knew there wasn't anything I wouldn't try if it meant I could get better. Then one day after my workout at the gym, Steve mentioned something he thought I should consider. He told me that maybe I needed to work on toning myself a little more, because the judges liked that slim, European look.

I weighed 85 pounds. Never in my life had I thought I needed to lose weight.

But I'm not going to blame Steve alone for what happened to me over the next couple of months. In fact, I don't think that it was his fault. Steve, Bela, and other elite coaches have often taken the rap for the eating problems and disorders in the sport.

But when Steve indicated that I should lose weight, I'm sure he was influenced by the results in England, just as I was. Like me, he was looking for any edge that might enhance my performance. Like me, he studied the girls who scored well at World Championships and realized that judges awarded the slimmer, more acrobatic girls.

Judges, not coaches, score gymnasts. And in the early 1990s, international judges thought that smaller was better. Tatiana Gutsu weighed 80 pounds when she won the gold in Barcelona in 1992. Shannon weighed 74 pounds when she won the World Championship in England in 1993.

And why did judges give awards to the thinner, more acrobatic girls? Because that's who the fans cheered. That's who the television announcers loved, long before any of us even were born. You can go all the way back to the 1972 Games, when the

Soviet Union's Olga Korbut was being called a "little pixie" on worldwide TV. Olga Korbut wasn't even the best gymnast at those 1972 Games—the taller, bigger Ludmilla Tourischeva won more medals than Korbut, including the all-around title. But the world fell in love with Olga Korbut because she was the little pixie. It was a subtle way of letting every gymnast in the world know that thin was in.

By the time my generation came along, gymnasts were getting smaller every year, and the tiniest girls were the most successful ones because they could most easily perform the difficult tricks.

Maybe Steve was wrong to talk about weight, especially after I was so desperate to improve after the 1993 World Championships. But like every coach I've ever had, Steve also emphasized that gymnasts should eat smart. USA Gymnastics also emphasized the importance of good eating habits and nutrition to elite gymnasts. No one ever told me to starve myself, and no one ever took food away from me.

Nevertheless, the ever-important triangle began to break down after my first few days back in Oklahoma City. After returning from England, I had moved in with the Webster family. Marianna Webster was a gymnast at Steve's and lived with her mother, Melanie Webster. I never really fit in, becoming more reclusive then, mostly because I became so determined in the gym. I still had my friends at Heritage Hall, but because I had missed so much schoolwork while I was in England, I spent most of my time studying. I kept putting more and more pressure on myself in every area of my life. On weekends I often stayed by myself in the house. At the same time, Mom was not visiting me as often because my grandmother was in the hospital in Chicago and Mom had to be with her. I also was not keeping in close touch with Sunshine. Then, when school let out, I wasn't doing as much with Rachel or any of my Heritage Hall friends.

I just sort of fell into a shell. And while I was in that shell, I decided to lose a couple of pounds. I found myself skipping meals and panicking whenever I ate something that had even just two or three grams of fat. I started checking out the fat grams in everything I ate. I would take just three or four bites of something before pushing it away. For breakfast, I would have a few bites of a fat-free muffin and then go work out from 8:00 A.M. until noon. For lunch, I'd have a few bites of chicken and rice before going to physical therapy and then working out from 5:00 P.M. until 8:00 P.M. And for dinner, I usually had just a cup of fat-free yogurt.

I didn't realize what I was doing to myself, and the Websters didn't realize it, either. High cholesterol counts ran in their family, so they watched their diets very closely. When they saw me skipping meals or nibbling on some fat-free food, it didn't seem out of the ordinary to them.

I figured I was just losing a couple of pounds. But then I started getting tired and weak. I focused on workouts because I knew that's where I had to perform. But I felt sluggish a lot more during the day and would feel completely exhausted at the end of the day. I never left the house and hardly ever read books or magazines anymore. I stopped doing my arts and crafts. I wasn't keeping a diary. I mostly just stayed in my room and slept when I was not at the gym.

Gradually, my body started to feel the effects of my poor eating habits. I had no more punch in my legs. I competed in an invitational meet against Ukraine and Belarus and did awful. I couldn't vault at all. I had no quickness or power. Steve was confused and upset. Tricks that used to be easy were now impossible.

A lot of people began telling me that I looked different, but I had no idea why they were saying those things.

Finally, Steve, Peggy, Shannon, and I were headed to the U.S. Olympic Festival in San Antonio. I was going to see my parents for the first time in nearly six weeks. It was the longest stretch I had ever gone without seeing them, and I missed them a lot.

But when Mom and Dad came up to my hotel room and I opened the door, Mom took one look at me and said, "Kerri, you look sick."

Dad said, "You're coming home with us."

Mom ran downstairs and found a drugstore, where she bought a bunch of vitamins and protein supplements for me to take. She was very worried. Dad asked about what I had been eating and how I was feeling. They couldn't believe how thin and weak I looked. When I saw my picture in the newspaper the next day, I realized they were right. You could see every vein in my arms and legs. I looked at myself and realized that I had overdone it.

"Kerri, don't ever do this to yourself again," Dad told me. "You're smarter than this. You know better."

And I did know better. But somehow I had lost touch with my family, my friends, and those things that helped me escape from gymnastics for a while. The triangle had broken down. My parents were upset with Steve that this had happened, but I was the one who fell into the trap that so many elite athletes have fallen into: desperation. I still wanted my dream more than ever. But I promised myself that I'd never be this desperate again.

Somehow I did really well at the Sports Festival, but I must admit I felt weak. Afterward, my parents were ready to take me home, but I convinced them that I would take control of my eating habits. I convinced them to let me compete at U.S. Championships.

But after the U.S. Championships, I went to a national team training camp in Atlanta, where USA Gymnastics trainers gave us our annual checkups. The trainers discovered that I hadn't just lost weight—I'd lost muscle mass and my body fat was down. They said that for a female, it was a dangerously low percentage. They gave me a lot of information about nutrition and told me to include more fat in my diet. They tried to have a heart-to-heart talk with me about training and eating the right way. But I was more concerned about putting together a good performance.

When I got back to Tucson for a week's break from Steve's after the National Training Camp, one of the first things I did was sit at the kitchen table and cut a big slice of cake for myself. Mom bought me one of my favorites, ebony and ivory cake, an absolutely decadent combination of white chocolate, white and dark chocolate mousse, and chocolate cake. It was delicious.

8

"God, please help me out"

✿

Mom and Dad were reluctant to let me go back to Steve's when my week at home was over. But we had a few long talks about keeping things in perspective. My mom planned to visit me more often, since my parents decided to move my grandmother, Mildred Monasee, to Tucson to keep better care of her. I also gained some weight while I was at home, and Mom and Dad spoke with Steve, who promised to keep an eye on things.

One condition of my return was that I not move back in with the Websters. My parents decided I needed a new environment. I moved in with the Smith family, who had a young son, Steven, who did gymnastics at a low level. My parents wanted me to avoid becoming consumed by gymnastics, as I had been when I had my eating problem. And the Smiths included me in many activities outside the gym, everything from going on company picnics to swimming, cooking, and shopping.

But one of the biggest reasons I went back to Steve's was because I had been invited to a few meets in Europe, including the prestigious DTB Cup in Stuttgart, Germany.

The DTB was in December, which was not quite three months away, so we decided I could stay at Steve's at least through that trip and then reevaluate things. When I went back to Oklahoma

City, I paid closer attention to nutrition and to what I ate when I was with the Smiths. I read all the information that USA Gymnastics sent me and a few other books on nutrition. The ordeal I had just been through helped me realize how easy it is for elite athletes, especially gymnasts, to be swept away by desperation if they don't have perspective and the right support system.

I became convinced that I began having problems in Oklahoma City not just because Mom couldn't come for as many visits and I lost close touch with my friends, but also because Aunt Ann and Uncle Don were not nearby for my weekend escapes. When I was in Houston, Ann and Don kept things normal for me by always being there. They had even a great influence on my eating habits, although at the time we were just having fun in the kitchen. Often Ann and I would spend time during my weekend visits cooking low-fat recipes from various cookbooks or even creating our own healthy dishes. We probably could put together a cookbook with all the things we made and the dishes we created—homemade soups, vegetable dishes, fish and chicken dishes. They were not only low-fat and healthful but delicious. Because of Ann and Don, even though I was away from home when I trained at Bela's, I never felt completely alone.

In Oklahoma City, even though I liked being with the Smiths, I really missed Ann and Don. I realized that no matter where I was, it was going to be a challenge to stay fit, healthy, and focused without Ann and Don's support. But I was determined to make the situation work.

During the first couple of months back at Steve's, I was training hard for the meets in Europe—the DTB, the Arthur Gander Memorial, and the Swiss Cup. They would give me some international experience against the next generation of Olympic hopefuls. But just as I was settling into a routine, doing fine in the gym and with the Smiths, I felt a slight pull in my stomach doing a set of pull-ups. My stomach was just sore, I thought. I finished the workout and took a couple of Advil. I didn't say a word about it to Steve, Peggy, or any trainer.

The next day the slight pain was still there. Then it got a little worse every day until everyone realized I was really hurting. I couldn't do any pulls or kicks on bars. Eventually I felt really bad, practically nauseous from the pain, whenever I tried to work out. But with the three meets in Europe coming up, I just wrapped an Ace bandage around my stomach every day and finished the workout. Whenever Steve asked me how I felt, I usually just shrugged and said, "I'm okay."

Mom came in to spend some time with me and when we went to get my stomach examined, the doctor said I had a badly pulled stomach muscle. He told me to take a minimum of a week off to let the injury heal. I nodded when the doctor told me I had to miss time in the gym, but in my mind I was telling myself, "No way."

I was doing it again. I was so desperate to reach my goals that I was losing perspective on how I should do things. This time I wasn't starving myself, but hurting myself. After sitting out one day, I told Steve I was feeling better and began training again. I also told my parents that my stomach felt better. In my heart, I knew I should have told people, "I can't go. I'm hurt." But I didn't.

There's a big difference between training in pain and training hurt. I was hurt.

I was just so proud and happy to be invited to those meets in Europe and so focused on my goal that I lost touch with reality again. Steve and Peggy realized I was nowhere close to my best.

They could tell from the hard time I was having in workouts that I wasn't ready to compete.

However, just a few weeks after injuring my stomach I was on a plane and on my way to Switzerland. I hadn't completed a workout in weeks. I hadn't done any of my full routines. Peggy told me we were taking a gamble entering the meets, but she said maybe I could rely on my experience to get me through the competitions.

At the Swiss Cup, which was a pairs competition on various events, I competed with John Roethlisberger. I made it through the early part of the program all right, but the real test was on bars, where you have to use your stomach muscles throughout the routine. When I began my bar routine, I could feel the pull on my stomach. It hurt, but I thought I could handle it.

But then, on a Kip—that same pull from the bottom of the bar to the top on which I tore open my knee as a child—I felt a big rip on my left side. I knew immediately that I had torn the muscle. It was like something was slicing my stomach in half, unzipping it from the bottom to the top.

Fortunately I finished the routine and it was the last one of the competition. But the pain was horrible. When I walked off the floor, I was hunched over, just trying to get out of there. I put ice on my stomach, clutching it with my hands.

"This is not good," I told Peggy.

Steve hadn't made the trip with us because he went to Australia with the Dynamo junior girls team. I'm not sure if Peggy knew how much I was hurting, but I rested the next couple of days and could hardly get out of bed. It was just like when I broke my sternum when I was ten. I had to rest on my side, then roll over and just sort of slide to the ground before I could pull myself up.

I knew I had no business competing in the Arthur Gander, but I felt guilty about having to tell Peggy that I didn't think I could go. I also didn't want anyone in the federation to think that I just gave up, that they sent me all the way to Europe and I didn't even compete. When we got to Montreux, Switzerland, for the Arthur Gander, Peggy told me that I was going to compete.

I began taking Advil, Tylenol, and aspirin—four and five at a time. I don't know how many I took in all, but I stuffed bottles and bottles into my gym bag. Then I did something I'm not very proud of now. I found a drugstore and bought an icing spray, an ethyl chloride solution that you spray on an injury to numb it for a while. I had seen foreign athletes use such sprays before. You can't buy them in the U.S. without a prescription, but you can in Europe.

I sprayed my stomach with ethyl chloride and figured that adrenaline would get me through the meet. When we got to the arena for training before the meet, I could hardly warm up, but I was spraying my stomach every chance I could. I was also taking Advil, Tylenol, and aspirin.

During warmups on the beam just before the competition began, I slipped and hit my leg. Because of all the aspirin I had been taking, my leg swelled up bigger than a softball. It started hemorrhaging because all the aspirin I had taken thinned my blood.

So here I was, spraying the ethyl chloride on my stomach, leg, and ankle, which had also become sore. Between every routine, I would dig into my gym bag, grabbing pills and the spray and trying to make it through the day. I just did my routines by instinct, by feel.

And I don't know how, but I actually scored pretty well. I couldn't possibly have looked very good in the competition, but at least the judges thought so. On bars, I couldn't pull up my legs at all because of my stomach. The entire routine, I just tried to keep my toes pointed and stick the landings. Somehow I finished fourth all-around.

By the time we were on our way to Stuttgart, Germany, for the DTB Cup, which was the whole reason I wanted to go to Europe in the first place, I just wanted to go home. At this point, I couldn't punch because of my leg and I couldn't lift because of my stomach. Some gymnast I was!

The DTB was going to be an events-only meet, no all-arounds, so that was a relief. I scratched from the vault because I couldn't run down the runway. I did bars and actually had the highest score through the preliminary round, although I had nothing left after that. On beam, I did a good routine, but couldn't pull out the double-back dismount. I had no punch. I landed on my face and got a nose burn. As I lay there on the mat, my eyes watering because of the pain in my nose, I thought to myself, "God, please help me out."

I stood up as best I could, walked off the floor, and slumped into a chair. I put my hands over my stomach and could feel a big divot where the tear was. I buried my face in my hands and started crying.

That was undoubtedly the lowest point in my life. Everything hurt. I was tired and numb, and I knew I never should have competed. I was doing with pain exactly what I had done with food—hurting myself.

I was doing things I knew better than to do. Like my dad told me, I was smarter than that. As we flew back to the United States for Christmas break, I realized that not much had changed in the year and a half since Barcelona. I still didn't feel any closer to my dreams. If anything, the things I did to myself while I was at Steve's pushed me further from my goals.

When we landed in Oklahoma City, Mom was waiting for me. After I hit bottom in Stuttgart, I called her and told her everything. She flew to Oklahoma City and already had some of my bags packed when our plane landed. I'll never forget the look of concern on her face the day I got back, the same look she'd had earlier when she saw how thin I'd become. She saw that I was in pain and was upset that I'd tried to compete when I was hurt. She said she was taking me home and her decision was nonnegotiable.

I never went back to Steve's after that. Steve called and spoke with my father, saying that he had things under control and he would keep a closer watch on me. But my father told him, "No, she's our daughter and we know things need to change."

The doctors did an MRI and found that I had a severe tear in my stomach muscle. I showed the doctor the big divot in my stomach and he just shook his head, as if to say, "Why did you do this to yourself?" To this day, I still have a lump of scar tissue in my stomach.

It was sort of a mixed blessing being home over the holidays. I spent three weeks hardly able to breathe without feeling the pain in my stomach. I couldn't do any sort of workout at all, couldn't even ride a bike. I had to roll out of bed every day, and when doctors told me it would be at least six months before I would be able to compete again, I was devastated. I had never spent six months away from gymnastics.

But the good news was that I was at home and would stay there. Since I wasn't working out, I quickly put on weight. I renewed old friendships: Katie Rose and I went to a lot of movies, went shopping, and did all the things I had missed. My mother and two of her best friends, Linda Ferlan and Marge Wright, gave me a lot of support, too, by taking me to events outside my gymnastics world. All of a sudden, I was outside my gymnastics career looking in, and I couldn't believe what I had done to myself.

After the holidays I enrolled at Green Fields Country Day School. For the first time in my life, I was a student—nothing else. When I was told it would be six months before I could compete again, I realized that it really had to be six months. I wasn't going to rush anything this time.

My father came home from work one day and handed me a sheet of paper. On it was a piece by Charles Swindoll:

Attitude

The longer I live, the more I realize the impact of attitude in life. Attitude, to me, is more important than facts. It is more important than the past, than education, than money, than circumstances, than failure, than successes, than what other people think or say or do. It is more important than appearance, giftedness, or skill. It will make or break a company, a church, a home. The remarkable thing is we have a choice every day regarding the attitude we will embrace for that day. We cannot change our past. We cannot change the fact that people will act in a certain way. We cannot change the inevitable. The only thing we can do is play on the one string we have, and that is our attitude. I am convinced that life is 10 percent what happens to me and 90 percent how I react to it. And so it is with you. We are in charge of our attitudes.

I taped that piece of paper to the mirror in my bathroom. Every morning I read those words. To this day, that piece of paper is still taped to my mirror.

I knew my attitude about my career and rehabilitation had to change. I was going to have to be patient. Being at home was the best therapy of all, and I was glad that it was only 1994. I knew that I could take my time and still be back in plenty of time to compete before the 1996 Olympic Trials.

USA Gymnastics was great about helping me along slowly. Through the first three months, Larry Nassar, a national team trainer, consulted with Bob Wallace, my physical therapist in Tucson, about my therapy. They put together a program in which I underwent various treatments and deep massages twice a day. I would sit in whirlpools and get electrical stimulation treatments. Debbie Van Horn, another national team trainer, was also involved. I was grateful that so many people showed so much interest in my comeback.

After three months, I finally got to go to the gym for the first time since the DTB Cup. I went to the same place where I first began my career, Gymnastics World, which had changed its name from the Gymnastics Center. And it was like I was starting all over again. I just did a few walks up and down the beam. USA Gymnastics sent Geza Pozsar to keep me motivated, and he was terrific. He came in from Sacramento and I practiced a few dance elements with him. I will never forget how much he helped me both mentally and physically. If Geza hadn't come to see me when he did, letting me know everything was going to be all right, I don't know where my gymnastics career would have led.

Jerry Hinkle, the Gymnastics World coach, consulted with USA Gymnastics and gave me a good program to start with. National team coaches Arthur Akopian and Muriel Grossfeld worked with me, too.

The process was so slow, but I knew I was doing things the right way. I relearned all the compulsory routines. I added some new elements. Until the doctors cleared me, all I could do was handstands and cartwheels, but gradually I forged a real bond with Arthur Akopian, who has a coaching style a lot like Mr. Gault's—quiet but efficient. Arthur calmly told me what I did wrong or right. Arthur is a former world champion, so he had been through many of the same experiences I had. His career was a lot like mine, also, because he'd been injured badly several times. So he knew to pace me. Arthur was the perfect coach for me at that time.

I told my parents how comfortable I felt around Arthur, so as I got closer to being cleared for competition, we decided to see if we could find a way for me to train with him permanently.

The only problem was I really didn't want to leave Green Fields, my old school, or my friends. My parents were also adamant about my staying at home. They decided to speak with Arthur about his developing a training program for me even though he lived in Los Angeles.

Eventually Arthur told my parents that he believed I could recover from the injury and become an Olympic champion. He spoke with federation people and everyone agreed on a plan for Arthur to commute to Tucson more frequently. My parents paid for Arthur's travel and accommodations and the federation helped pay his coaching fees. I was worried about all the expense, but my dad said flying Arthur in was cheaper than when I lived away from home.

Arthur developed a program for me that Jerry Hinkle helped me with on the days Arthur wasn't in Tucson. Things worked out well when I began going full speed in the gym. Before I knew it, I felt stronger than I had in more than two years. During the workouts, I slowed down when I needed to slow down and I went hard the rest of the time. And there were no shadows anywhere in sight. I realized I didn't need Kim or Shannon to push me. Arthur was a great teacher, Geza was helping with my choreography, and Jerry Hinkle was very dedicated and put in many extra hours. Together, we made a great team.

By the summer of 1994, I had entered my first meet. It was just a zone meet in California. However, I did really well, winning every event and the all-around. We were two years away from Atlanta and I never felt or looked better. I was back.

Two weeks later, I entered the U.S. Classic in Palm Springs, which was going to be my first real test. Dominique Dawes, Amy Chow, and Amanda Borden were a few of the big names that were going to be there, but I was predicted to win it.

Before I left, NBC came in and did a few interviews with me, Mom and Dad, and Arthur and Jerry. They were planning to do a story about how much I had overcome in my career and how I was back in top shape.

They even sent a camera crew to the U.S. Classic to get some footage of my big comeback meet. But I never saw any of that video. I couldn't bear to watch.

9

"I want to know if she's ever going to be able to have a family and hold her children in her arms"

❊

People always ask me why I put up with everything, why I subject myself to so much pain and heartbreak. Especially after I suffered my stomach injury, people asked why I'd continued my career when I knew better than anyone that there were no guarantees in my sport.

But they just don't understand. I can't explain the thrill I always have felt when I'm flying through the air, spinning and turning, performing at my very best. When I hit the mat, plant my feet, raise my chin, and throw out my hands in the finishing pose, it's the greatest adrenaline rush in the world.

Anyone who ever said I was giving up too much because of gymnastics just doesn't understand. Gymnastics has given me so much more than I can ever give back.

That's why I climbed all the way back into top shape by the time the U.S. Classic rolled around in early August 1994. I was in the best shape I had been in for more than a year. My stomach was fine. I wasn't hurting anywhere, either physically or emotionally. I was at home with my family and about to enter my senior year at Green Fields Country Day. I was eating right and was healthy. I had many good friends and had carved out a nice, if still circumscribed, social life for myself. I was even planning to participate in a Cotillion, a sort of debutante ball, later in the year around the time I turned seventeen. Imagine that—me, whose entire life had been spent in leotards, wearing a formal gown and being presented to society by my father. I felt confident about everything in my life. And on top of everything, the Atlanta Games were no longer a distant dream, but were just two years away. I felt ready for anything.

Arthur, Geza, and Jerry were good for my gymnastics, too. I had new routines and tricks on every apparatus, and the difficulty levels were higher than ever. On floor, I was doing a double layout back, which I hadn't done since early 1993. I had a full-in on my last tumbling pass, which was a somersault with a full twist, a difficult trick with which to end a program. On beam, I was doing a punch-front, which was a nice standing front somersault. I had new choreography on my floor, thanks to Geza. I was feeling that special thrill, that adrenaline rush, every day. Sometimes at practice when I really nailed a trick or routine, I would just shout out loud—"Yes!"—and bounce over to the next apparatus ready to keep going.

When Mom and Dad flew with me to Palm Springs for the U.S. Classic, I was feeling happy about every aspect of my career. Even though I hadn't competed but once since my stomach injury, lots of people had noticed how strong and confident I was. Before the U.S. Classic, coaches and gymnastics people were predicting that Dominique Dawes and I would contend for the all-around title. Shannon was not in Palm Springs because she was at the Goodwill Games with Steve, but Amanda Borden, Amy Chow, and Jaycie Phelps were some of the more well-known gymnasts also competing. I was excited just being there, because I felt as though I had been away from the top of the sport for so long. I also knew that this represented a big step on the way to World Championship Trials, so the timing of my comeback was perfect.

When the U.S. Classic competition began, I was nervous, of course, but I had so much adrenaline rushing through my body that I was confident I would do well. And sure enough, I hit my compulsory floor and vault routines. I was in second place, just behind Dominique Dawes, and all that was left for the day was bars and beam.

Compulsory bars has never been my favorite event, but usually I've been able to complete it without any major breaks. I have never been the best in the world on bars, but over the years I got to be pretty consistent. I was always able to do whatever it took to finish my bar routine without suffering mandatory point deductions.

When I got to the event, Mom and Dad were sitting nearby, just twenty feet from the apparatus. They were proud of how far I had come since my stomach injury. We were competing at the Palm Springs Convention Center, in a sort of exhibition hall. Since it was not a big arena, the fans were very close to the athletes and noise echoed off the walls. You could hear the fans clearly whenever they shouted encouragement: "Come on, Kerri. . . . Let's go, Dominique."

I was hoping for a real strong start on bars, because one thing that separates bars from all other events is that you have to rely much more on establishing a flow in your routine. On floor or beam, if you slip early, you just get back up and finish. On vault, the entire routine is over in only a matter of seconds. But on bars, if you have a break early, getting back into the rhythm of your routine is usually difficult. Since so much of a bar routine relies on the speed and momentum generated from giant swings, when you have to start all over after a break, it's difficult to get that speed and momentum back. You also have to have a certain feel, or flow, during a bar routine, or you can suffer the consequences.

From the moment I started on bars, things were not quite right. I fell out of synch on my first handstand on the high bar, over-rotating. Then I overcompensated as I tried to get back vertical on the bar. I was fighting to stay straight and to catch up to where I needed to be in the routine. Everything was just a little bit off. When I got to a critical part of the routine, where I do a slip-grip maneuver and then hop from the high bar into a handstand on the low bar, I probably should have taken an extra swing on the high bar to regain the speed and momentum I had lost earlier.

But I didn't want to receive the mandatory three-tenths deduction the judges would have given me had I taken an extra giant swing. I thought I could pull out the tricky slip-grip, which is a move that requires you to quickly shift the position of your hands on the bar while swinging into a handstand. I thought I had enough speed and strength to make the move and get to the low bar.

But when I tried to shift my hands, I already had swung too far over the bar and lost my grip. The momentum of my body sent me flying and flipping toward the low bar and the floor. Instinctively I tried to reach for the low bar and catch myself before I crashed, but I smacked my face on it instead. I was going too fast. In a flash, my chin and chest smashed into the floor, and because my body was still rotating very fast, when I hit the mat, my body jackknifed in the wrong direction. I twisted into a backwards C position at impact, my heels whipping back and hitting the back of my head—an awkward, ugly fall.

I lost all my wind and felt a sting shooting up my back and down my legs. Then there was a tingling in my legs, and for a moment I didn't think I could move. I tried to roll onto one side and just gasped. I was so scared.

"Help me, somebody, help me," I said as I lay on the floor gasping and crying. I could hardly breathe and knew that something drastic had happened to my back. The convention center fell completely silent. All you could hear echoing off the walls were my words: "Please, somebody, please."

Arthur and three or four trainers rushed to me. One trainer said, "Okay, hold her still. Kerri, don't move. It's your back."

My father ran to the floor and bent over me. "Kerri, you're going to be all right. Don't move right now. Kerri, we'll take care of it. You're going to be all right."

My mom stood to one side, her hands over her mouth. I heard her say, "Kerri? Kerri? Are you all right?" She just stood petrified, staring at the trainers, coaches, and my dad as they worked on me. Ever since that moment, my mother has never been able to watch me compete without getting physically ill herself. Watching me hit the mat the way I did terrified her.

Dad and the trainers helped the emergency medical team put me in a neck brace and roll me onto a gurney. I was on the ground staring at the ceiling and wondering what was wrong with my back for at least fifteen minutes. It felt like hours. As they began rolling me to the ambulance, Mom and I stared at each other, both of us upset that something like this was happening once again.

A few coaches and USA Gymnastics people circled around me and kept trying to encourage me. "Come on, Kerri, hang in there. You're going to be fine, Kerri."

Someone put his hand on my father's shoulder and said, "Dr. Strug, don't worry, she'll be fine for the U.S. Championships."

That was the wrong thing to say. My father is one of the most even-tempered people you will ever meet. I could count on one hand the number of times I have seen him lose his temper.

But that day was one of those times. The only reason gymnastics was ever important to my father was because it was important to his kids. His number one concern is his children. When that person mentioned the next meet as I was being wheeled out of the hall, with none of us knowing how severe the injury was, my dad just snapped.

"I don't care about any gymnastics meet or anything but Kerri right now," he said, raising his voice. "I don't care if she ever walks into a gym again. I want to know if she's going to be able to walk. I want to know if she's ever going to be able to have a family and hold her children in her arms."

Mom and Dad rode with me in the ambulance to Desert Hospital. I had feeling in my legs throughout the ordeal and believed that I could move everything all right. The tingling I felt in my legs was only for a brief period, right after I hit the floor. In the ambulance, I felt more of a sting in my back; it just felt out of place. But Dad and the EMTs were very concerned and were not taking any chances. When you injure your back, one wrong move can make it much worse, possibly even lead to paralysis. I wore the neck brace and lay perfectly still all the way to the hospital.

As I lay there, I kept telling myself, "Oh, God, please make it all right. I'm going to be all right."

When we got to the hospital, I underwent various tests, X-rays, MRIs, and CAT scans and was given some strong pain medication. I was in a room with my parents when a doctor came in and told us that I had a stress fracture in the area of the L-4 and L-5 vertebrae.

At first I didn't know if that was good news or bad. Stress fractures? I'd had stress fractures in my legs before and been back in the gym two days later.

But this was my back. I had heard of some people with stress fractures in their backs having to have rods inserted to support the spine, obviously ending their careers and affecting their lives. We talked for a while about the possible consequences of my injury; luckily it didn't seem to affect my nervous system.

Dad saw the test results, and he and another doctor compared the X-rays with previous X-rays of my back. They talked about how the stress fracture was probably there before my fall, but the fall made it worse. I told Dad that I remembered my back being sore when I was at Steve's, but I had never felt real discomfort. And during my training with Arthur, I had no back problems. Nevertheless, I was experiencing another setback. Just as I was feeling so good about everything in my life, I was literally on my back. Finally I asked how long the injury would keep me out of the gym.

"Probably six to eight weeks," the doctor said.

Another eight weeks? I felt betrayed by the sport I loved.

"Well, I guess that's it for me," I thought to myself.

Several times before that day, I had said I wanted to quit. I had thought about it and wondered about it, but I always knew that what I really wanted was to keep going. Everyone thinks about quitting sometimes. It's only natural. But I usually only thought about it when I was tired, sore, or discouraged. As I lay there in the hospital bed, I thought it might finally be time to quit.

"I'm cursed," I told Dad.

I was fitted with a bulky back brace and stayed in the hospital for two days. I was there not so much because of my back, but because I had recurring dizzy spells. Almost every time I stood up, I fainted. When I finally got over the dizziness and began feeling better, I went home. My back still hurt, but the thought of going through another eight weeks of therapy hurt me more. I wondered if this time I should just finish school and get on with my life. Earlier, I had been contacted by UCLA gymnastics coach Valorie Kondos and was offered a scholarship to compete there. Competing in college was one of my goals. I wondered if that was the direction I should go in, forgetting about my Olympic aspirations.

But as soon as I got back home, Arthur and a lot of federation people called me, checking on my health and encouraging me to try another comeback. They talked a lot about how much the sport needed me, how much my country needed me, and how much I had overcome already. I received a copy of the NBC video of my fall, but refused to watch it. To this day, I still haven't seen it. I had so many high hopes for that meet, but it just led to more pain and confusion.

Throughout those first few days back home, I often woke up in the middle of the night with severe back spasms. Every muscle in my back would cramp and spasm. I would slowly get out of bed and work out the spasms by walking a little bit. And as I walked up the hall to the bathroom, I always saw that verse about attitude that I had taped to the bathroom mirror. Every morning when I woke up, I would look at it again.

One part stood out: "We cannot change our past. . . . We cannot change the inevitable. The only thing we can do is play on the one string we have, and that is our attitude."

I realized that I could never change what had happened in Palm Springs, Orlando, Oklahoma City, Stuttgart, Barcelona, or anywhere else along the path I had traveled. I realized I couldn't change the inevitable. But what had always pulled me through before was my attitude and my family and my love for the sport. All of those things that had kept me dreaming were still there after my back injury.

So I decided, again, to keep dreaming. The first step back, as always, was just getting myself healthy again. The brace I wore through the first two weeks after my fall was very bulky. Constant spasms in my back kept me from walking normally for a while. After a couple of weeks, I switched to a less bulky brace and began more serious therapy.

Bob Wallace, Larry Nassar, and Debbie Van Horn developed a comprehensive physical therapy program. This time the therapy involved a lot of deep massages, ultrasound treatments, and exercises in a swimming pool. I tried to do a little more every day, riding a stationary bike and doing exercises and stretches. I became very determined to make it back in time for the World Championship Trials, which were just six weeks away. If I wasn't at school, I was usually doing some sort of physical therapy or exercise. All day, every day.

The one big meet my stomach injury had prevented me from competing in earlier in the year was the individual World Championships in Brisbane, Australia. I was very upset about that, because I hated missing a world championship and Australia is one place I have always wanted to see. So I targeted the Team World Championships in Dortmund, Germany, as a meet in which I wanted to compete. I didn't want to miss another world championship. Team Worlds were in November, just over three months after my fall. More important, World Championship Trials were in late September. I was going to have to really work hard and hope for a little luck, too, if I was going to make the team.

I began going to therapy with Bob Wallace twice a day. I was willing to try anything if someone said it might speed up my recovery. I even got Mom to talk to the people at Canyon Ranch, a resort and spa in the Tucson area, and they allowed me to use their wave pool, a therapy pool designed to stimulate your muscles. I went there and used it as often as I could. While I was at Canyon Ranch, I also tried shiatsu, Jacuzzis, herbal massages, and even acupuncture. They pierced me with needles everywhere—my ears, arms, back. I don't know how much it helped, but I was willing to try.

Something that definitely worked were my visits with Dr. Jean Williams, a University of Arizona sports psychologist. I began seeing her about once a week shortly after my back injury, and we really saw eye to eye on a lot of things. We discussed attitude, positive thinking, and focus. She convinced me to set small goals and work my way up from there. She taught me a lot about being realistic with my goals and not comparing myself with others. She was someone with whom I could really communicate.

By September, Arthur and I were again working in the gym. I had switched to a smaller back support, something like a weightlifting belt. Later, I worked with a neoprene support belt and began doing full routines on everything but floor, where the constant pounding was too hard on my back. I still wasn't 100 percent and probably did do too much too soon, but, yes, I managed to make it onto the World Championship team. In fact, much to my surprise I placed second overall at the World Trials. It was my fourth world team and I was thrilled and proud to qualify because I knew the hard work and dedication necessary to make that team. I also knew how many people helped me achieve that goal.

I wore the neoprene brace until the day before Team Worlds began in Dortmund, Germany. I knew I could make it through the competition and score well, even with a watered-down floor routine. But there was one huge hurdle I still had to overcome: compulsory bars.

I have to admit, I was nervous. The first time I did the slip-grip after my fall was in practice before World Trials. It probably was the most difficult part of coming back, but we stacked several mats on the floor and I practiced the slip-grip dozens of times. I also pulled it off well at World Trials, but I still was thinking about it at the World Championships. I kept telling myself that what happened in Palm Springs was a freak accident. I thought about all the times I had done bars without a mistake. And I remembered a lot of the things Dr. Williams and I had talked about. I went through my routine step-by-step in my mind before the meet began. I closed my eyes and did a drill that we talked about, telling myself key words that took me through the routine: tight, strong, stretch, swing.

After warmups, I told myself, "You've worked too hard to fail. You can and you will have a great performance."

And when the light came on and it was time for compulsory bars, I made it through the slip-grip. I spun to the top of the bar, changed my grip, and whipped into a perfect handstand on the low bar. It was a big moment for me, but probably only a handful of people in the arena knew it. It took a lot emotionally to get through that move. Maybe because I was so relieved to complete the slip-grip, I lost my concentration for a moment and on another move in the routine one of my hands slipped on the bar. I scored only a 9.487, but considered it a victory because I made it through the slip-grip and was having a good competition.

I hit everything else in compulsories, and after the first day we were in second place behind Romania. A lot of people thought we wouldn't be able to hold that position after optionals, however, because Shannon had shin splints, so Steve pulled her out of the meet. Steve's decision meant there was no margin for error for the Americans. Every one of our routines was going to count, and we had a very inexperienced team. I had been on four World Championship teams and Dominique Dawes had been on three, but the rest of the team included Amanda Borden, Amy Chow, Jaycie Phelps, and Larissa Fontaine, none of whom had a lot of senior international experience.

We also were considered the underdogs because neither Steve nor Bela was there to coach us. Mary Lee Tracy from Cincinnati Gymnastics was named head coach of the team, and she lacked an international reputation. But let me tell you, Mary Lee did an incredible job. She instilled great confidence in each of us. With Shannon injured, Mary Lee was counting on Dominique and me to lead the team.

That's why I still consider those 1994 Team Worlds a turning point and a real confidence booster for me. My team and my country needed me, and I did not disappoint. Dominique and I led the way to a silver medal. Romania finished first and Russia was third. It was the first time a U.S. gymnastics team ever defeated a team from the former Soviet Union in a major competition.

I felt like my comeback was complete. I had performed at my best in an important meet. I had finished eighth in the world with my all-around score. Even before returning to the United States, I began developing a new plan, with the 1996 Olympic Games at the top of the list. I took the UCLA letter of intent with me to Dortmund, and after the competition I signed it and faxed it back to Valorie Kondos. I was going to be a Bruin. When I got back to Tucson, I talked with Mom and Dad about what I wanted to do over the next year and a half. I planned to graduate from Green Fields in June and, prior to enrolling at UCLA, take a year off from school to concentrate on making the 1996 Olympic team. I knew the year off wouldn't affect my academic progress too much because I was graduating a year early and was still making straight As. After the Atlanta Games, whether I made the 1996 Olympic team or not, I would go to UCLA and compete collegiately. That was the plan.

Over Thanksgiving break I spent time with my family and then went to the Cotillion and had a great time. I danced with my dad and he was so proud, showing me off in my formal gown. But as 1994 quickly became 1995 and my back began feeling better, we kept working on developing just the right plan to make the big final push to the Olympic Games. I knew in my heart that the next year and a half would be tension-filled but thrilling. Things could only get better. I mean, what else could go wrong?

10

"Holy cow, he's really back"

❀

People say things always work out for the best. The two years of my struggle with bad luck and injuries made me a believer. When I walked across the stage with my high school diploma in my hand on June 5, 1995, I realized that despite nearly two years of pain and many setbacks, being at home for that critical time in my life had been *very* good for me.

I was with my family. I'd had a normal high school life. I realized how many people really cared about me. My friends and teachers were great, and so was Arthur. But with high school over, I knew that if I was going to make the 1996 Olympic team, I had to find a gym where I could get all the training I needed. The Olympic Games were barely a year away and Arthur found it hard to continue commuting. "It's just one year," I thought to myself. "I can handle anything for just *one* year."

And so our first project after graduation was finding a gym that could help me reach my dream. I really hadn't competed very much since the Team World Championships, partly because of school, partly because of my back, and partly because of a ruptured eardrum. I had gone to bed one night in December feeling ill and woke up the next morning with my ear throbbing and red fluid staining my pillow. The ruptured eardrum affected my equilibrium for a long while, making it difficult to balance in handstands and walkovers, so I simply tried to stay in shape. Arthur continued to give me as much coaching as he could, but his busy schedule made it hard for him to come to Tucson and give me the time in the gym that I needed.

I had been hearing rumors that Bela might return to coaching in order to help Kim Zmeskal in a comeback attempt, but I hadn't talked with Bela or Kim and didn't take the rumors too seriously. Mom and I decided to visit Mary Lee Tracy's Cincinnati Gymnastics, after having been so impressed with the way she handled the 1994 silver medal World Championships team. I thought I would like it at Mary Lee's and I knew she was a good coach. A big part of me wanted to go there. Tom and Lori Forster's program in Colorado Springs was also recommended to us, so Mom, Dad, and I went to see the Forsters' Colorado Aerials team.

We decided that I should join the Forsters, because Colorado Springs was much closer to Tucson than Cincinnati. It was a nice way to ease back into a regular competitive routine away from home. And by being in Colorado Springs, I had access to all the U.S. Olympic Committee's facilities and physical therapists at the Olympic Training Center and headquarters.

Tom and Lori were top-level coaches, but they didn't have a lot of international experience. When I joined their gym, it was the first time I ever felt like a real "veteran" in the sport. Tom and Lori were coaching a lot of young girls and were somewhat new to the senior international level themselves. Training with me in Colorado Springs were Doni Thompson, Kristy Powell, and Theresa Kulikowski, all of whom were talented gymnasts with bright futures. But they were all just coming out of the junior national ranks. I realized that the training environment I was accustomed to was different from what I was getting from

Tom and Lori. Their emphasis was on technique rather than on conditioning and intense training. As the days passed and we still were not working as intensely as I thought we should be, I got nervous. Several big meets were fast approaching and the Olympics were only a matter of months away. I made suggestions to Tom and Lori in practice and asked about a timetable for adding new tricks to my routines.

But Tom and I just never developed the appropriate coach-athlete relationship. It wasn't his fault or mine. It just didn't happen. For a while, it was a lot like when I was training as a junior elite. Practice would end and most everyone else would leave the gym, but I would stay late and work on conditioning, dance, or something else that needed extra attention. After all I had experienced in the years before joining the Aerials, I knew what it would take to get me to the Games, and I didn't believe I was getting it in Colorado. Don't get me wrong: Tom and Lori have a top-quality gym and do an excellent job with many athletes. It just wasn't right for me.

Tom told me one day, "I'm sorry this isn't Bela's."

And I thought to myself, "You're right. It's not Bela's."

Still, I very much appreciated Tom and Lori helping me get to some big competitions in the summer of 1995, including the Olympic Festival, where I won the all-around and uneven bars competitions and took third on the beam.

By late July, when we were back in Colorado Springs training for the U.S. National Championships, I was hearing more stories and reading articles about Bela's return to coaching. He was helping Kim try a comeback and coaching thirteen-year-old Dominique Moceanu, who had become a phenom in the sport.

I knew Dominique well from my stay at Bela's. She was always talented, competitive, and an excellent junior. She and Jennie

Thompson, the girl whose family I lived with in Houston, were predicted to be at the head of the next class of Bela's girls. But Jennie had moved on to Steve Nunno's after Bela's retirement in 1992, while Dom stayed at Bela's and trained with other coaches as she worked her way up the ladder.

Both Dominique and Jennie were impressive gymnasts with stars in their eyes. One day before the 1992 Games I was signing autographs with Dominique at an event and I saw her writing '96 *gold, for sure* as she signed her name. Now, *that's* confidence.

By the summer of 1995, Dominique had indeed won just about everything at the junior level and was stepping up to the senior elites for the first time. The 1995 National Championships were going to be her first-ever senior national meet. For me, it was going to be close to my thirtieth major national or international meet.

When we got to New Orleans for the meet in August, I went to the arena for training the day before the competition began. By then, I knew Bela had made a comeback. But it was incredible to see Bela coaching for the first time since the 1992 Olympic Games. There he was, just as if nothing had changed and no time had passed. He was tugging on his shirtsleeves and hunching his shoulders as he always did when he was nervous. He looked the same as ever, stalking the floor like a tiger. He was moving heavy equipment like it weighed nothing. He was tightening the wires on the apparatus and placing the vaulting board perfectly into place. He looked like a surgeon working with the equipment. I saw Martha, too, and heard them speaking with their Romanian accents. It all looked and sounded so comforting and familiar. Before Dominique began a practice routine, Bela put his hands on her shoulders and stared into her eyes to tell her something. I could imagine exactly what he was saying. "Stay strong. Sturdy. Confident."

It was eerie. There I was, having experienced so much in the sport and grown into a real veteran, but I still felt in awe of Bela. Until I saw him, it was as if Bela's comeback wasn't real. But I quickly found out at those national championships that Bela's presence and the impact he had on Dominique was definitely real.

Dominique was awesome throughout the competition, accomplishing something incredible when she won the individual all-around in not just her first senior national championship, but her first senior meet. She was crowned the new American star right there in New Orleans, with just a year to go before the Olympics. She was already casting a big shadow in the sport. I finished fifth in the all-around, third on bars, and fourth on the floor. I saw Dominique compete so successfully and knew that she was training more intensely than I was. I realized that Bela and Martha had not lost their touch.

Someone asked me after all-arounds what I had to say about Bela's return. I responded, "Holy cow, he's really back."

When we returned to Colorado Springs to begin preparing for World Trials and the 1995 World Championships, I felt I wasn't getting all the training I needed. I wasn't taking all the necessary steps toward Atlanta. I was competing with just one vault in my repertoire, and at big international meets, you have to have two. I felt like I was falling behind. I asked Tom and Lori about adding a second vault, and we briefly worked on one in the pit. Tom and Lori did a good job of getting us ready for World Trials, and in the end, the Colorado Aerials qualified three girls for the World team—Doni Thompson, Theresa Kulikowski, and me. Mary Beth Arnold, Shannon, Dominique Moceanu, and Jaycie Phelps also made the team. Tom and Lori were experiencing success at the world level. But I knew that there was someone in Houston who didn't have to learn how to get me to where I wanted to go. Bela already knew how to get me to the Games. He already knew what I needed.

I finished fourth all-around at World Trials and made my fifth World Championship team. It was something I was very proud of, because at that point Shannon and I were the only Americans ever to make as many as five World Championship teams.

We arrived in Sabae, Japan, for World Championships in October, and the Japanese held an elaborate reception for us and gave us colorful robes and gifts. Shannon and Dominique were popular stars in Japan. Everyone knew them. I thought the trip to Japan and the way we trained together was great for USA Gymnastics. We were a *team* again, getting along and working well together. We were less than a year away from Atlanta and wanted to make a statement going into the Olympic year.

We didn't quite reach our goal of winning the gold at Worlds, but we took the bronze and were excited about the direction we were heading. After all, we had a lot of young girls on that team and Dominique Dawes and Amanda Borden could not compete because of injuries. Personally, I came away feeling confident that I had the ability to reach all my goals in Atlanta. But I also felt that I might need to leave the Forsters if I was going to achieve those goals.

Even though I made all-around finals for the first time ever in a World Championship, eventually finishing seventh overall, I was still somewhat frustrated with certain aspects of my training in Colorado. It was my fifth World Championship team, but Tom and Lori's first. The whole time we were preparing for Worlds and competing, Tom asked me a lot of questions about what to expect and how things were done at Worlds. I was used to the coach having total control in those situations. And on vault, Tom asked me to try a vault that I had done only in the pit during training. I had never competed with it or even practiced it outside the pit. With all the injuries I had sustained, I was reluctant to compete with a vault that I hadn't perfected.

Meanwhile, the whole time we were at Worlds, I saw Bela taking full control of the competition like he did at National Championships. I saw the way he walked into the arena and took care of everything down to the last detail. I saw him stalking the floor and motivating Dominique. I thought to myself, "Whoa, what am I doing?"

After all-arounds, Bela and Martha both congratulated me and told me I looked good. They were very encouraging.

When I spent a week at home after Worlds, I talked with Mom and Dad about wanting to go back to Bela's.

"Well, you really need to think about this. You know how tough it's going to be," Mom told me.

Dad said, "It's your decision. You know what you want better than anybody else."

I put our reliable twenty-four-hour rule into effect and thought hard about my decision for a day. Actually, I thought about it for several days and still felt the same. If I was taking the year to concentrate on training for the Olympic Games, I wanted to go for it all the way. I wanted the best. I wanted to go back to Bela's.

In early December, my mom called Martha and told her that I wanted to come back to Houston. They talked for a long time and my mom and dad made it clear that much had changed since I was thirteen. They spoke about everything I had experienced since 1992. My parents indicated that they hoped Bela and Martha would stay positive with me and would monitor my nutrition and health. I spoke with Bela and Martha, too, and also let them know that things were different now. They promised to be more understanding and accommodating.

Tom was not pleased when I decided to move to Houston, but I tried to make it clear to anyone who asked that I just felt Bela was right for me. I didn't want my move to be a reflection on Tom and Lori. Tom still criticized me publicly and hurt me very much when he went on national television and said, "One thing we knew when Kerri came here was she certainly displayed the ability to leave."

That really hurt. I always had a good reason for leaving a gym. I left Bela's when he retired, Brown's when the Browns separated, Steve's primarily because of my stomach injury, and Gymnastics World because it became so difficult for Arthur to continue commuting.

Nevertheless, I had trained at four different gyms since I'd left Bela's, chasing my dreams the whole way. Through it all, no place I went ever was like Bela's. Sunshine talked about a special bond Bela and I had. She said we both were incredibly dedicated and strived for nothing less than the best.

And ever since Barcelona, part of me always did wish that Bela would come out of retirement and help me get where I wanted to go. Sunshine was right: I always wanted to be in Houston, where I would go through the grueling workouts, tumble on that hard floor at the ranch, learn from Bela and Martha, and feel that special thrill whenever they helped me stick a new trick or perfect a new routine. I wanted to feel the soreness, bemoan the long, lonely days, and be pushed to the limit. One thing I *never* felt when I trained with Bela and Martha was unprepared.

When I got to Bela's in December, I was almost relieved to know that the next six months were going to be tough. I wanted to step into that gym and start the hard work. Interestingly, I again was stepping back into the shadow of another big-name gymnast.

This time it wasn't Kim or Shannon who was the big star, but Dominique Moceanu. She was already doing endorsements, making appearances, planning a book, and appearing on the cover of magazines. Bela tried to regulate all the attention Dominique was getting, hoping to avoid the pressures that had affected Kim in 1992, but it was hard to do.

As soon as I arrived in Houston, I was amazed at the change in the way Bela and Martha treated me. They really respected my opinions and treated me as a peer.

I had a much better relationship with Martha. She was still very tough in the gym, but she and I spoke much more often and communicated much better. From the first day I began training with her again, Martha kept telling me, "You have to talk with me. Are you doing okay? You have to tell me how you're doing."

Our relationship was totally different the second time around. Before, to be honest, I was afraid of Martha. I used to hate practicing beam every day because that was Martha's domain. But during my second stay at Bela's it was as if Martha and I reached an understanding. If I told her I needed an afternoon off, she realized that I really needed an afternoon off, I wasn't just tired of workouts. The same was true with Bela, with whom I have always had a special relationship. He trusted my judgment much more.

They paced me really well and were bending over backwards to accommodate me. I don't think it was just because of the talks my parents and I had with them, either. I think their retirement changed them. They seemed much more at peace with themselves.

But don't think for a second that their workouts were any easier. They were not. In the gym, Bela was still in charge. I had to do what Bela and Martha said in the gym, like always. Hard work was one of the biggest reasons I went back to Houston in the first place, and hard work is what I got.

Beginning with the first practice, workouts were as grueling as ever: running, drills, sit-ups, jumps, and long hours. We did conditioning and compulsories for hours in the mornings, optionals and new tricks in the afternoon, and choreography and private instruction at night. I was in the gym at 7:30 in the morning and home from the gym at 8:00 P.M., with naps and physical therapy in between workouts. Not much had changed from my last stay at Bela's. Everything was a test again. Everything was strictly business.

An interesting group was training with Bela when I first arrived. There was Dominique, the young one, but then there was Kim, myself, and Svetlana Boguinskaia, the former Soviet superstar. My first thought when I saw Svetlana at Bela's gym was "What's she doing here?" Svetlana was a former all-around world and Olympic champion, and for a long time she was a real rival of American gymnasts.

With the 1996 Olympics just a year away, Svetlana moved to Bela's for the same reason I did—to get the toughest, best training. Svetlana was a beautiful lady and had been competing for Belarus since the breakup of the Soviet Union. At twenty-three, she was trying to make her third Olympics. She is a hard worker, and contrary to what many of us thought when we competed against her, she is a lot of fun, with a good sense of humor. Svetlana always competed with a serious expression on her face, so she could be very intimidating on the floor. But she and I hit it off right away. I really liked her.

The first few weeks at Bela's were made easier because Arthur was there, visiting from California and helping Bela. Geza was also there helping out. I caught myself looking at the people around me during practice quite often. There was Kim, Svetlana, and Dominique, a pair of world champions and the reigning national champion. I looked at the incredible coaches who surrounded me—Bela, Martha, Arthur, and Geza, who have accounted for more medals than some countries will ever win. And I thought to myself, "This is why I came back here. For me, this is the best coaching staff and environment in the world."

I knew I was back at Bela's when we got just two days off for Christmas. I spent the holidays at Ann and Don's, where I lived until moving in with the family of a gymnast at Bela's, Amanda Seholm. The Seholms lived near Bela's gym, which made it easier for me to rest between practices. We were working out twice a day, which I hadn't done in nearly two years. I was a little out of shape since I had some time off after Worlds and we never really worked as intensely in Colorado. I was very sore during the first few days, but Bela and Martha paced me well and the results of training there quickly became apparent.

I learned a lot of new tricks and combinations and finally got that new vault I had been wanting. It was the Yurchenko 1½, which I hadn't successfully completed since 1993. It was one of the most difficult vaults in gymnastics and my favorite in the world, because of the risk, challenge, and possible high scores involved.

The Yurchenko was first successfully completed in 1983 by a Soviet star named Natalia Yurchenko, who earned the distinction of having the vault named after her. It is a vault in which the gymnast sprints full speed down the runway and just before hitting the vaulting board does a round-off. She somersaults onto the vaulting board and then pushes off with both feet, gaining great height as she somersaults again onto the horse. As she pushes off the horse with her hands, she begins rotating her feet toward the floor, completing a 1½ twist. It can be magnificent watching a gymnast stick a Yurchenko, but it is also a very risky maneuver.

But just one month after arriving at Bela's, I had all my confidence back and I was nailing the Yurchenko 1½ every day. Bela said the way I was performing the Yurchenko, it was going to carry me a long way. I had no idea how right he was.

11

"I am Kerri Strug"

❀

I think Bela could sense a change in me as much as I saw one in him. The "scared little bird," as he called me before 1992, wasn't intimidated by the bright lights of a big competition anymore. The confidence I had as a gymnast was becoming more evident with every routine I did. I think the transformation actually began at the 1994 Team World Championships in Dortmund, when Dominique Dawes and I helped an inexperienced U.S. team win the silver medal. Gradually I kept getting more and more confident. By the time I finished seventh in the individual all-around finals and helped us win the team bronze at the World Championships in 1995, it was apparent to everyone in the sport that I no longer left my best routines in the practice gym.

There were a lot of reasons why. By spring 1996, of course, I had grown up so much. I understood how to compete and could focus only on myself during meets. Dr. Williams was a big help. My family, like always, was a big help, and I was finally healthy and strong again. But more than anything, I had come to the realization that no matter what I encountered on the gymnastics floor, I had already seen it all. I knew I could overcome anything I faced, because I already had overcome more than most people would ever have believed. I was eighteen.

But in terms of gymnastics, I was a hardened, experienced veteran.

I had chased my dreams from competition to competition, from coast to coast, and all over the world—Holland, Germany, Switzerland, Japan, England, France, and Spain. Through the many pitfalls of the sport, the many second- or third-place finishes, and the injuries that were supposed to end my career, I kept chasing my dreams. Through the emotional lows, living in the shadows of the superstars and staying with eight different host families in five different cities, I had survived and had a chance at the 1996 Games. I had known the styles and criticisms of Bela, Martha, Steve Nunno, and half a dozen other elite coaches. Nothing on the gymnastics floor scared me anymore.

Bela told the press: "I see something happening. This fragile-looking kid is lion-hearted. Kerri is coming out of her shell."

The only obstacle left for me to overcome was winning. I had not won a major international individual competition since I was a junior elite. Through more than five years of senior competition, I had finished in second place more often than I cared to remember. I had finished third, fourth, and fifth lots of times. I had contributed greatly to the improved standing American gymnastics had around the world, but when I flew with Bela, Martha, Svetlana, and Dominique Moceanu to Fort Worth in late February for the McDonald's American Cup, I still had never won. It was the only thing on my mind.

The American Cup was a major international competition less than five months before the Olympics. Forty gymnasts from twenty-two countries were invited, including Svetlana, who was competing for Belarus. Dominique was also going to Fort Worth, but just for interviews because so many media people wanted to do a story about her. Dominique wasn't going to compete because of a heel injury and lingering pain in her shins. Shannon wasn't going to compete, either, because of a problem with her wrist, so the American Cup was getting as much attention for who was *not* going to be there as for who was. Still, for me everyone knew it was a big meet.

When we arrived at the Tarrant County Convention Center the day before the meet, Bela and Dominique went to one corner of the floor and did interviews for at least an hour with a big group of reporters. Svetlana was cornered by another group of reporters and talked for a long time about training with Bela and being one of the favorites to win the meet. Martha and I quietly went through warmups and workouts, moving from apparatus to apparatus practically unnoticed. When I was finally finished, I sat on the floor near the bars and spoke with a couple of reporters. They asked me about having something to prove in the American Cup meet. Bela walked up and they asked him about me.

"Kerri, she has nothing to prove to anyone," Bela said. "Yes, she easily could win here and go on and win in the Olympics. But she has already had a great athletic career. She has done more than many athletes and has been through a lot. I hope she does win, because she deserves to have the light shine on her face. But she is already a champion."

One day later, it was time to prove it. Ever since I rejoined Bela's in December, we really hadn't competed very much. This was another indication of how Bela and Martha had changed since 1992, when we went through so many competitions in such a short period of time that we hardly had anything left for Barcelona. Bela knew we had peaked a little too early in 1992, so he was pacing our competition schedule much better in 1996. After the American Cup, we were going to skip the World Championships in Puerto Rico in April and also skip a couple of other competitions. The plan was to show our new skills and routines early in the year and then peak for National Championships and the Olympic Trials in June. I thought it was a good plan, but it also meant I had to make the most of the American Cup. It was going to be a big step toward Atlanta.

On March 1, 1996, the morning of preliminaries, I decided it was time to start a new diary. Through all the hard times of 1994 and 1995 I had stopped keeping a diary, but this was where my Olympic dreams were getting so close. I needed to talk about it.

"Hey, remember me?" I wrote. "I thought I would start another diary since it's another Olympic year. It's time to come into my own. I've been doing my routines so consistently for a month now. It's time to show everyone how far I've come. It's my turn to shine."

I started the night off on vault and nailed a Yurchenko Arabian, which is like the Yurchenko 1½, but with only a half twist. It was automatic, just like in practice. I also went through bars and beam with solid routines. Going into the final event, the floor, I barely trailed Oksana Chusovitina from Uzbekistan for the overall lead. Oksana hit her vault on her last event, and Svetlana, who was in third place, bobbled a little bit on her floor routine. Then I stepped up as the final competitor of the night. I was trying my new floor routine for the first time in a competition. And I nailed it. The tumbling runs were strong. The whole routine was explosive and crisp, with the crowd clapping in unison as the music played and I bounced across the floor. I finished with the highest score of the night, a 9.775. I performed with much more emotion and energy than ever before, and the crowd noticed. I definitely felt a bond with the crowd that I really had never felt before. I smiled and waved, and when I was done and ran off the floor toward Bela and Martha, Bela looked at me, thrilled, and said, "You did it! You did it! This is the best I have seen you."

I was 77.3 feet away from my dream.

I missed the Yurchenko for the first time in more than six months. Worse, I felt a horrible pain in my left ankle.

I heard a rip, like Velcro, shoot up my leg. I was in excruciating pain.

Team trainer Barb Pearson and Martha help me off the podium after my second vault. I was screaming in pain, but I kept asking Martha if the judges counted my vault as a fall, since I collapsed after saluting them.

Moments after hurting my ankle on the vault, I'm under the stands, being told that we won the gold. I was happy, but in so much pain. And I was confused, because I didn't think I would get to go to the medal ceremony.

I spent virtually every moment after the vault trying to get my ankle better for individual events. Here, I'm getting ultrasound, but both Martha and I knew my individual hopes were a long shot.

Even though my vault had people calling me "the next Mary Lou," all I really wanted was to compete in all-arounds and event finals. This picture was taken moments after Bela told me my Olympics were over. I still had my leg elevated, hoping some miracle would happen.

During the *Time* photo shoot the day after team finals, I found a way to keep my foot elevated. I just kept hoping that somehow I would get to compete again.

The day after winning the gold in 1996. There were so many
photographers taking pictures, our heads were spinning.

A moment I'll cherish forever.

With Hillary Clinton at the president's fiftieth birthday party.

We liked the George Washington bust at the White House
so much that we decided to make him part of the team.

With Lisa Fernandez and Shaquille O'Neal, before going on the
Today show. Lisa and the USA softball team adopted me when
none of my gymnastics teammates went to the Games' closing
ceremonies. I sat with the softball team and had a great time
watching the show.

My hero and friend Nadia Comaneci surprised me by coming to my nineteenth birthday party at Planet Hollywood in Los Angeles a few months after the 1996 Games.

I'm backstage after winning the 1996 ESPY for the best performance under pressure. One of the "clutch performers" also nominated was Tiger Woods, and I thought he would win. I was just happy to be sitting there with so many great athletes.

My mom and me, with the Champ at the Hugh O'Brian Youth Foundation Banquet in New York. Mr. Ali was always smiling, and he hugged me. I was touched and honored to meet him.

I was at Planet Hollywood in New York with my mom and Lisa when I told someone at the restaurant that I'd love to meet Sylvester Stallone. They called him on the set of a movie, and he said he wanted to meet me, too. "You mean he knows who I am?" I asked. I had no idea how many people saw the Olympics.

I helped out Arnold Schwarzenegger with one of his favorite projects, the Inner-City Games, and he called me "champ."

With Bruce Willis, the night of the vault. Everything was a blur.

With my mother a few days after the vault. We were in a daze because
of all the attention I was getting.

At home with my dad after Atlanta. He's been such an inspiration to me.

Lisa and me at a UCLA football game after I'd started college in September of 1996.

Later, we talked about this being the first time in my life I had come from behind to take over a meet. I was in first place going into the next day's all-around finals and I wrote just one thing into my diary before going to bed: "Tomorrow I'll remain calm and I'll do it."

And I did. It was my first individual victory ever as a senior elite. After more than thirty national and international meets over more than a five-year span, I finally felt what it was like to walk up to the top step of the medal platform. What a feeling! I won every event in the all-around competition and ended on the floor routine with a 9.837, which was the highest score of the entire weekend.

"You've been waiting for this night a long, long time," Bela told me. "You are a totally new person. You have come such a long way."

He and Martha were so excited for me. Sunshine and her mother came to the competition and they were just bubbling over with excitement, too. Mom and Dad were so proud. I knew some people were going to discredit my victory because Shannon and Dominique were not there to compete, but I didn't care. I knew what I had been through to get there. I felt it was the last little confidence booster I needed. I was a winner. Svetlana finished second and Oksana Chusovitina of Uzbekistan was third. I won $5,000 with the title, but I didn't take the money because I still wanted to keep my amateur status. Besides, how could I put a price on what I had just experienced in Fort Worth?

When we got back to Houston, we moved out to the ranch, which has never been my favorite place in the world. I hated being so isolated and immersed only in gymnastics. But I was happy and confident after my win and pushed myself hard every day at the ranch. Just as when I was thirteen, it really helped when my mom could come visit me. Often she would come with her best friend, Linda Ferlan, who is like a godmother to me, and they always helped ease the tension.

By late March, Kim realized she could not make the comeback that everyone hoped she would. She stopped training with us. A couple of weeks later, Svetlana had to leave to train with her team in Belarus, so Dominique and I were the only ones left in the gym.

Bela added a third workout to our schedule, so we did stretching, running, and conditioning from 7:30 to 9:00 A.M., then optional routines on every apparatus from 11:30 to 2:00, then compulsories and more running and conditioning from 5:00 to 8:00 P.M. It was the same schedule every day, except Saturdays, when we had only two workouts and it got to be very difficult to handle. Basically I worked out, took a nap, worked out again, took a nap, went to physical therapy, worked out again, slept. Time just sort of ran together. Whenever I felt like screaming, I kept telling myself to make it through only that one day. The next day I would try to make it through just that day, and so forth. Each day was a competition in itself. I began counting down the days until Atlanta, writing the number in my diary. But at least I still had my regular Sunday visits and walks with Ann and Don; they became a real escape for me.

In late April, Bela finally gave us a break, and I went home for thirty-six hours. My time in Tucson went by way too fast. When we got back to the ranch I was once again counting the days until the Olympics. "Being out here at the ranch makes me tired mentally and physically," I wrote on May 20, 1996. "I can't get away from gymnastics, ever."

But then we made it to the first week in June, when the big Olympic push and important competitions began. First came the

USA Gymnastics National Championships, which were going to qualify the top fourteen gymnasts for the Olympic Trials three weeks later. Even though we had been working so hard in the two months since American Cup, we were peaking at just the right point. Before leaving for Knoxville, Tennessee, for the National Championships, we had a verification in front of the campers and I hit everything, including both Yurchenkos.

Once we got to Championships, I could have scored a little better overall, but I confidently hit my routines except for a fall on optional beam when I tried a new mount. I was happy finishing fifth, behind Shannon, Jaycie Phelps, Dominique Moceanu, and Amanda Borden. I qualified for my second Olympic Trials. I wrote in my diary on June 8, 1996: "I hit everything. This is going to be a very good Olympic Team, I think."

It already was becoming clear that experience and talent were definitely going to be on our side in Atlanta, if no one suffered a serious injury. Shannon, with her wrist, and Dominique Moceanu, with a stress fracture in her right leg, were having the hardest time getting over injuries. After qualifying for the Trials, they both scratched from the apparatus finals at Championships. Amanda and Jaycie also scratched with minor injuries, which meant that of the top Trials qualifiers, Dominique Dawes, who finished sixth at Championships, and I were the only ones who competed in everything.

Still, I liked the possibilities for our Olympic team and the direction in which the sport was headed. In Barcelona in 1992, five of the seven U.S. Olympic gymnasts were sixteen years old or younger. We also averaged 4 feet 9 and 83 pounds in Barcelona. But of the top six finishers at National Championships in 1996, only Dominique Moceanu was younger than seventeen, only Dominique Moceanu and I were not at or near 5 feet tall (I was

4 9½), and our average weight was closer to 90 pounds. Shannon, Amanda, and Dominique Dawes were all nineteen. I was eighteen. I thought the age and experience of our best gymnasts brought a lot of integrity back into the sport, after gymnastics had been criticized so much in 1992 and 1993. And even as older, more mature girls, we still managed to keep a lot of difficulty in our routines, although this led to a lot of nagging injuries.

The worst injuries going into the Trials were those suffered by Shannon and Dominique Moceanu. I knew firsthand from watching her in practice every day that Dominique's shins were bothering her. She had been so celebrated in the months leading up to the 1996 Trials. Her situation was a lot like Kim's in 1992, with Dominique suffering from a bad injury at a bad time. I also could tell from the competitions in which I saw her that Shannon was having a hard time with her wrist. For me, what was beginning to hurt a lot was my left ankle and shin. My right shin hurt a little bit, but I could feel the constant strain in my left leg.

Shortly after we got back to Houston after Championships, Bela rearranged our practice schedule again, cutting practice back to two a day. But he added a workout on Sundays, which meant my trips to see Ann and Don were over. I wasn't real pleased. It was a lot of work with no rest. One day a thunderstorm knocked out all the power at the ranch, but Bela still had practice in the dark gym. I knew my body needed at least one day a week in order to rest and recuperate, and I cherished those days at Ann and Don's. I decided to talk with Bela and Martha about it, which I never would have done before. I told them I thought I needed to take a day off. It was then I realized how much my relationship with Bela and Martha had changed. They agreed. Just ten days before Trials, they told me I probably was right and gave me the day off. They trusted my judgment; this made me feel great. "I needed this," I wrote in my diary after returning to the ranch from a day at Ann and Don's.

My shins were beginning to hurt a lot. I was working hard and pushing my body to the limit, and I never got a break in the gym because by early June, I was really the only one working out. Dominique was not doing much at all because of the stress fracture in her leg, so I had Bela and Martha all to myself. Geza and Arthur also came in to help, so there were four coaches and me.

Larry Nassar was visiting for a couple of days in order to treat Dominique, so he looked at my legs. He thought I had only sore tendons and muscles. He left some therapy machines at the ranch and showed me how to use them. But two days before leaving for the Olympic Trials, I wrote in my diary, "I'm really hurting right now. The pain in my shins and tendons won't go away."

I constantly told myself, "Don't let it affect you. Don't let anything stop you now."

Except for the pain, I was doing well. I was close to my dreams and I was hitting everything every time. Bela and Martha couldn't believe the consistency and strength with which I competed. Before Trials, we had another verification—just me, with all the campers and coaches watching. It was nerve-racking, but I hit everything. Just before that verification I found out that neither Shannon nor Dominique was going to be able to compete at Trials. USA Gymnastics decided to let their National Championship scores stand as their Trials scores, so Shannon and Dominique were basically petitioned onto the Olympic team. "It looks like there are just going to be five spots open at the Trials," I wrote in my diary.

I got to Boston on June 26 and felt like I was the one to beat, whether there were five spots open or one. We checked into our hotel, and when I got to my room, I lay back on my bed and opened my diary. "I can do these routines easily now," I wrote. "It's showtime. I'm going to be calm and confident. All my moving around, the long workouts, taking the hard road. It all comes down to this weekend. I want to make it all worthwhile. I'm ready. My left ankle is really hurting. It's the tendons, I think. But I can block it out. I can and I will do awesome this weekend. Get ready to hit everything, Kerri."

Just as at the American Cup, the athletes who were not competing in Boston were getting more attention than the ones who were. In the days before the competition began and even after we had started, Shannon and Dominique Moceanu were interviewed again and again about their Olympic hopes. They were shown on national television, watching our routines or talking about Atlanta. The rest of us just wanted to make sure we got to Atlanta. Of the athletes who were competing, there were a lot of talented girls who looked strong—Amanda Borden, Amy Chow, Dominique Dawes, Jaycie Phelps, Jennie Thompson. Everyone there had a legitimate chance to make the team. The atmosphere was intense, as always, like no other meet in the world. At Olympic Trials, if you don't hit your routines, it's the end of your dream. Years of training come down to one weekend. In Boston, falling apart physically and emotionally would be easy.

But as the compulsory competition began, I couldn't believe how calm and confident I was. I visualized every routine in my mind and then went out and hit every one of them. I ended the compulsory program on the floor, and when I finished, the roar of the crowd had my skin tingling. I scored a 9.887, the highest score of the night.

Two days later, I was four routines away from making my second Olympic Team. I was nervous all day. I still hadn't seen

Mom or Dad, because I liked to keep to myself at major competitions. My left leg was also still hurting and I could feel and see the tension in Bela's face.

When we walked into the FleetCenter, the whole place was buzzing. Shannon and Dominique sat in a skybox again, doing interviews and watching the rest of us try to earn one of the five remaining spots on the team. I looked for Mom and Dad in the stands during warmups, and when I found them, I felt much better. I began the night on vault, which was another relief. It was my favorite event and I still hadn't missed a Yurchenko in months. When the green light at the end of the runway flashed, telling me to begin my routine, I suddenly didn't feel as nervous anymore.

I saluted the judges, sprinted down the runway, hit my marks perfectly and did my round-off entry into the vaulting board. It felt perfect. I reached back to the horse, pushed off, whipped my legs over, twisted 1½ times, and planted my feet into the mat. Everything was perfect. I scored a 9.95 and whispered "Awesome" to myself as I saw Bela throw both his fists into the air and shout, "Yes, yes, yes." It would prove to be the highest score of the night.

By the end of the competition, not only had I made the Olympic Team, but I had the highest all-around optional score of anyone. I hit all my tumbling runs. I had the beam routine of my life, scoring a 9.825. Coaches were telling me I had never looked better. The crowd was great, cheering wildly and making me feel wonderful.

I was an Olympian again. Shannon and Dominique came down to the staging area, changed into USA warmups, and joined Jaycie, Amanda, Dominique Dawes, Amy, and me in a locker room underneath the stands. We laughed together and congratulated each other on making the Olympic team. A lot of USA

Gymnastics people were moving in and out, congratulating us and telling us to get ready to march back into the arena for the official introduction.

What an incredible night! We walked onto the floor and the noise was deafening. The song "Proud to Be an American" blared through the speakers, and I'm sure there never have been seven athletes more proud to wear the red, white, and blue than we were that night.

We were given flowers and marched around the arena again, smiling and waving as lights and cameras flashed in our faces. At the press conference afterward, so many people asked me so many questions that it was all a blur. The seven of us sat together for a formal press conference, and then we were interviewed individually. There were lights and cameras everywhere. I think we all realized right there that the attention we were going to get before the Games was going to be like nothing any of us had ever experienced.

Someone asked me about the difference between being on the 1992 team and being on the 1996 team. "The goals are definitely higher now," I said. "And since we're going to compete in the United States, there are high expectations."

Bela could not have been more complimentary about my performance. I think he realized that because Shannon and Dominique were getting so much attention, NBC and a lot of the fans and the media hadn't really noticed that I scored the highest on the optional routines.

Bela told the reporters: "It is special to coach Kerri. She thinks differently about her athletic career than 99 percent of the others around the world. She does it for herself and the pride of her country. For so many years, Kerri has been in the shadows of the great ones. I hope in Atlanta she gets the spotlight. She deserves the spotlight. I hope you know she was great tonight. She came here and was so much different than before. Her head was up, her eyes were bright. She was saying, 'Look at me. I'm the best. Here I am. I am Kerri Strug. I am the one who is a winner.'"

After about an hour, Bela and Martha went into a meeting with the other coaches and the USA Gymnastics people. They were going to name a head coach for the Olympic team. As we waited, I got to see my family and we celebrated together. When Bela and Martha came out of the meeting, I was stunned to hear that Martha had been named head coach of the Olympic team, with Mary Lee Tracy. I just assumed the coaches would be Bela and Steve, but it was a nice gesture for USA Gymnastics to finally give Martha her due. Bela was very proud of her. It turned out to be a perfect night for Bela's girls—Martha included.

I didn't get back to my hotel room until very late that night, but I did pick up my diary and start writing: "The relief I feel is indescribable," I wrote. "I am a two-time Olympian. I still can't believe it. I have been through a lot since I was in Barcelona, but I've landed on my feet. What happened four years ago motivated me to keep going, and I'm glad I did. I've almost reached all my dreams. Now I have to win a team gold, an individual all-around medal, and an event final medal."

12

"Even if I have to carry you, you're going out there"

❀

I don't know when or where I first heard our 1996 team described as the Magnificent Seven. But it was a very appropriate nickname, and not just because of the talent the team possessed. Sure, when we went from the Trials to a pre-Olympic training camp in Greensboro, North Carolina, I looked around and could see the potential of our team: Shannon, so experienced and talented, especially on beam and bars; Jaycie, who had come a long way since making her first world team in 1994 and was very consistent, especially on bars; Dominique Dawes, a powerful tumbler with a lot of experience, including the 1992 Games; Amy Chow, great on bars and vault; Dominique Moceanu, the 1995 all-around national champion; and Amanda Borden, a great competitor who was always solid on the beam and floor.

But beyond what I could see on the gymnastics floor, it was magnificent the way we instantly bonded with one another off the floor, too. In one week of training together in Greensboro, we became closer and more of a team than we ever did in 1992. Martha and Mary Lee were great at defining exactly what our roles were going to be. Everyone's opinion mattered to them, whether you were an athlete, a coach, or a federation official.

They convinced us all that the greatest goal was a team gold. Martha told us we could think about our individual goals only after the Olympic team competition.

We also were building friendships with one another as we traveled and trained together. Just as in 1992, we had all spent a lot of time competing fiercely against each other before the Olympic Trials. But curiously, the very time we spent competing with one another drew us closer together, because we knew what we had all been through. We had all spent years waking up before daylight, taping our ankles and wrists, chalking our hands, practicing two or three times a day. We had all grown up making sacrifices, counting the days until our next trip home, counting calories. We all had twisted ankles, torn blisters, jammed wrists, sprained fingers, pulled muscles. And some of us had overcome very serious injuries. We had fallen down a thousand times, but we always got back up. We heard our coaches yell at us until we cried. We worked and worked on one little move, one tiny part of one routine, until finally we got it right. We moved in with host families in strange cities and made homesick calls to our parents and friends.

We all knew what the life of an elite gymnast was like, and that bond drew us together. We were also more mature as individuals. Amanda, with her unselfish team spirit, was voted team captain.

This year, too, politics never entered the picture. Coaches and federation people got along great and understood each other. I think USA Gymnastics, especially Kathy Kelly, deserves a lot of credit for doing things the right way from the very start in 1996. I think USA Gymnastics also changed a lot between 1992 and 1996. The Trials procedures were spelled out clearly before we ever took the floor. Every last detail about our training and preparation for Atlanta was planned perfectly.

The federation and Martha and Mary Lee also announced that the starting lineup for the Olympic rotations was not going to be based on an athlete's reputation or on what the coaches thought, as it was in 1992. Politicking was going to be taken out of the equation. The lineup was going to be based on results from the National Championships and the Trials. In other words, this time I would compete last on vault and floor because I won those events at Trials.

Everyone looked happy, prepared, and healthy throughout the week. Shannon was over her wrist injury. Dominique's stress fracture was just about healed. My left leg still was sore, but I thought it was nothing that would hinder me.

We were doing everything together and supporting each other, and this made us stronger as gymnasts and friends. At practices we helped each other out and then went together to a lot of special events planned for us. We had dinner together, socialized, and were really very relaxed throughout the training camp. I couldn't believe how calm Bela was. He was laughing and very loose all the time. Our every move was being chronicled by the media and followed closely by fans and we just got closer and closer.

We closed the week with a pre-Olympic exhibition. At our last workout before the exhibition, 600 reporters showed up to interview us and take pictures. While an unbelievable amount of attention was focused on us, we just took it in stride. We were getting calls from agents, fans, sponsors, public relations people. Reporters, television cameras, and fans were following every move Shannon, Dominique Dawes, and Dominique Moceanu made like never before. The federation was planning a post-Olympic tour during which each of us was guaranteed up to $100,000, but I kept saying no to the idea of turning professional.

The crowd at Greensboro Coliseum went nuts with every routine we did, and I couldn't have imagined a better send-off to Atlanta. I was the only one who did full routines on all four events. Each of the other girls skipped at least one event because they didn't want to aggravate injuries. The end of the show was an extravagant finale and send-off, with fireworks, a huge American flag dropping from the ceiling, patriotic music blaring, and the crowd cheering us wildly.

We hadn't seen anything yet. Atlanta was like a big, beautiful carnival, the biggest Olympic Games in history, with so many people from all over the world coming together for those "16 Days of Glory." I was glad USA Gymnastics shielded us somewhat from all the craziness, providing us with accommodations in which to live and train in seclusion—another smart decision.

It was a big secret at the time, with a lot of media and fans always asking us where we were staying during the Games. We lived in, of all places, a fraternity house, the Connally House at Emory University. It was a beautiful redbrick house with six two-story columns along a huge front porch and a lush green front yard. There was plenty of security, too, with a guard at every door twenty-four hours a day and the house cordoned off with police tape. There was a nice living area where we spent a lot of time together. We even had our own cooks, nice ladies who made all our favorite healthful dishes. Each of us had our own room, with a telephone, a television, and plenty of space.

I brought with me only the official USA outfits that the USOC provided for us and a few pairs of shorts and T-shirts. I brought a camera that I definitely knew how to work; this time I wasn't going to ruin the pictures if I got a chance to meet the Dream Team. I brought a teddy bear from home and some gum. And of course I brought my diary: "I am so excited and ready for the Games to begin," I wrote. "Mom and Dad, Lisa and Kevin, and so many people I love are here to support me. This is going to be an incredible experience."

Sunshine came to the Games on a break from summer school at UCLA. Ann and Don flew in from Houston. Even Patty Exum and her daughter Kelli, my friends from Orlando, bought Olympic tickets and came to Atlanta to see me. Kim was there. So were Mary Lou and Nadia, my heroes and friends.

"Kerri's always been the bridesmaid," Mary Lou told the world press at a pre-games press conference. "This might be her time to shine."

I felt so ready. We trained at the Tucker Gymnastics gym, about twenty minutes outside of downtown Atlanta, which was also nice. We weren't distracted by crowds or the media, so we accomplished a lot in those days before the Games. On July 20, it was estimated that more than three billion people turned on their televisions to watch the elaborate opening ceremonies of the Twenty-Sixth Olympiad. Unfortunately, I was one of them. Just as in 1992, because the compulsory program began the next day we could not go to the opening ceremonies. I was on my second Olympic team, but still waiting to go to my first ceremony.

I was honestly thrilled watching it on TV, however. I was ready and motivated for the competition to begin before the opening ceremonies, but watching the U.S. team march in made me even more excited.

The next day we had breakfast together and an easy morning workout. We went back to the house to rest, but we were all restless. We finally boarded the vans that would take us to the Georgia Dome and hardly spoke a word to each other. I'm sure everyone else was thinking exactly what I was thinking: Just hit.

I couldn't believe the energy we all felt from the crowd at the Georgia Dome. When we marched in for team compulsories, the place erupted in noise. We warmed up and then began the competition on bars, and there was never a doubt that this was a special American gymnastics team. I was second up, which was a little strange because I was going to be last on vault and floor, but I hit a good routine and gave us a nice score—a 9.675. Everyone hit on bars, and when we got to the beam, everyone but Jaycie hit their routines again. Jaycie fell and scored just a 9.012, but only the top five scores counted, so we were fine.

We went to the floor trailing only Russia and Romania, our longtime rivals. We were still trailing when I stepped up on the floor as the final competitor in the rotation. I hit everything crisply and confidently, and when my score of 9.825 flashed on the scoreboard, 32,000 people screamed and applauded because it pushed us past the Romanians into second place. We marched to the vault, and again, there was not the slightest slipup. When I stepped up as the final competitor of the rotation and got the green light from the judges, I sprinted down the runway and hit my vault for a 9.812. It was the highest score we got on the apparatus and pulled us to within .127 of a point of the Russians overall.

We were one day away from the first Olympic gold medal in U.S. women's gymnastics history.

After dinner the night before team finals, I went up to my room and opened my diary. "Everyone was really pumped up today," I wrote. "Martha and Mary Lee lined us up and gave us the lineup for tomorrow's optionals. They told us how this was our last team workout. This is it. We're capable of winning."

We were confident that we could make up the difference, especially with the loudest 32,000 people I've ever heard cheering everything we did at the Georgia Dome. Those were great crowds. I'll never forget the emotion I felt every time I walked into the stadium. I wish I could hug and thank every single person who supported us with American flags, red, white, and blue outfits, and cheers.

As I continued to write in my diary the night before team optional finals, I turned on the TV and watched the U.S. men's team finish fifth overall in their team finals. That was a pretty impressive finish for the men, who were not expected to contend. I knew the supportive American crowd had helped the U.S. men perform beyond most people's expectations. The crowd would be a big boost for us, too, I was sure.

"Tomorrow's going to be our turn to show the world how good the U.S. women's gymnastics team is," I wrote. "I'm going to be the second one up on bars, third on beam and last on floor and vault. I just have to hit those routines. I want the gold. I want to make individual finals. I stuck everything in both practices today, but I didn't do the vault in the evening practice because we all felt like we did enough in the morning.

"Well, it all comes down to one day. I know I'm prepared and capable of doing all my routines great. I've done them so many times before. I just need to do a few more. As for the team, we're all ready. We're going for the gold. We just need to hit. Well, gotta go. Go USA! We can and we will be awesome tomorrow."

On the morning of the team finals, Martha and Mary Lee talked to us about what each of us had been through on the way to that point in our lives. When she said that, I tried to think about everything I had experienced. They told us to be aware that we were on the brink of making history. They told us to perform like we always have performed. I had an easy morning workout and skipped the vault again because my left leg was still hurting and Bela thought I had done the Yurchenko enough.

Just before leaving my room to board the vans on the afternoon of July 23, 1996, an overcast and muggy day, I opened my diary one more time. "Kerri, you can and you will have an outstanding performance. Show the world how hard you've worked."

No one spoke on the ride to the Dome, except Dominique Dawes, who asked if someone could be sent back to the house to pick up her official USA athletic shoes. We were supposed to wear official warmups and shoes everywhere we went, but especially on the awards stand.

"I'm not going to be the only one on the awards stand not wearing shoes," Dominique said. We all forced a nervous laugh.

We got to the Dome, went through warmups, and fed off the energy from the crowd. I walked up to Dominique Moceanu and said, "Well, here it is."

"Let's hit everything," she said.

And that's exactly what we did. From the moment the first green light flashed and we started on the parallel bars, we hit everything.

Jaycie, me, Dominique Moceanu. Stick, stick, stick.

Amy, Dominique Dawes, Shannon. Stick, stick, stick.

It was incredible. Nobody scored lower than a 9.787 on bars. Shannon and I had been on more Olympic and World Championship teams than any American gymnasts in history—eleven between us since 1991. And I never had seen a U.S. team look so focused and prepared. We were at our best. The Russians were looking good, but we made up all the ground on them and took a slight lead in the first rotation. All the nervousness was gone. For me, it was like a big, beautiful verification out at the ranch, with 32,000 of my closest friends screaming support the whole way. Sunshine, Lisa, Kevin, and a lot of other family members were watching from a skybox. My mom and dad were sitting just a few rows off the floor. I found them in the stands, as I always did, and they looked more nervous than I was.

We were fantastic on bars, but we knew the balance beam, which was up next, would be the difference between us and the Russians one way or the other. Our coaches were incredibly fidgety as we marched toward the beam. As a team it probably was our weakest apparatus. For me, it was my least favorite, but I had been hitting beam quite regularly before Atlanta. I always approached the beam like a mechanic—piece by piece, just putting it together. But probably because of my better relationship with Martha, I had come to appreciate it and enjoy it much more.

I was the third one up for us on beam, because the coaches knew I could put up a good, solid score from which the three girls behind me could earn even higher scores. The strategy worked perfectly for us, too. Amanda and Jaycie were clean before my routine and then I put together a very nice 9.737, which is about as much as I could have expected. Dominique, Dominique, and Shannon were awesome behind me.

After the beam, the crowd was roaring nonstop celebrating our lead over the Russians. I breathed a big sigh of relief, really glad the beam was over.

Now I was confident. I knew the floor and vault belonged to me. I never said it publicly, but it's what I always felt. And all that was left between us and the team gold was floor and vault. It also was all that was left between me and the goal I had been chasing my entire life. I was sure I could come up with the scores to finally earn a spot in the individual all-arounds. Just as in 1992, only the top thirty-six athletes were going to make the individual all-arounds, but no more than three from the same country. With Shannon and Dominique Dawes performing so well, it looked as if it was going to be between Dominique Moceanu and me for the final individual spot.

When I stepped up to the floor, for the first time in my life I wanted all the pressure on my shoulders. I wanted it all to come down to me. I was the most confident person in the world. After all I had been through, I wanted the spotlight on me.

And before I knew it, I was in the spotlight. Our floor routines were going very well, but the Russians were still coming on strong. Then Shannon, of all people, bobbled on her routine and scored a 9.618. As I stepped up onto the floor as the last performer, I walked past Shannon. I could see the great disappointment in her face. And worse, as I stood there ready to begin, there was a delay in posting Shannon's score. Apparently, one judge had scored Shannon much higher than the other judges and the discrepancy had to be ironed out. Shannon's scores took forever to come up. As I stood there, shaking out my legs and stretching my arms, I started to lose my adrenaline rush. The crowd began chanting and clapping in unison. I started to get nervous. I looked toward Bela. He furrowed his eyebrows, hunched his shoulders, stared at me confidently, and mouthed the words, "Strong, Kerri. Stay strong."

I had heard Bela say those words a million times before. But just like that, I was intense and ready again. By the time Shannon's score was posted and the green light came on, I was the only competitor performing in the building. All the other rotations were done. Everyone watching the competition knew that I needed to hit my routine in order for us to keep our lead. Some of the Russian, Romanian, and Ukrainian coaches and a lot of athletes watched me out of the corners of their eyes. Finally, the spotlight. Finally, the pressure. Believe it or not, I loved it.

And more important, I performed as if I loved the pressure. The music began playing and I just started having fun. I hit every tumbling run, every move. I could hear the crowd clapping and cheering, and it just made me better. I never got tired. I felt stronger with every step I took.

"The little spark plug," Bela called me when I first arrived at his gym in 1990. That's what I felt like. When I finished my routine, I waved to the crowd and couldn't help but laugh out loud. I saw Bela throw both fists into the air and scream, "Yes, yes, yes! Go, Kerri! Go, Kerri."

Martha and Mary Lee greeted me at the bottom of the stairs and gave me big hugs. Shannon put her arm around my shoulders and said, "Thank you. You saved us." Dominique Moceanu hugged me and said, "You were *strong*."

It was a 9.837. We started feeling the gold. Even with Shannon's minor slipup on floor, my score helped us increase our lead. All that would keep us from winning the gold would be if we had some falls on vault. And that just never happens. Never ever.

But was I ever wrong. Even as we marched toward the vault apparatus, things were beginning to unravel. Some of the girls hadn't gathered together all their equipment and had to rush back to the floor area. I had to put on my vaulting shoes as we were walking toward the warmup, bouncing on one foot to put on a shoe, then bouncing along on the other. We lined up in front of the judges in the wrong order, which maybe only I noticed. We always were supposed to be tallest to shortest, and I was a stickler about those things.

Then as we began warming up, things got stranger still. During the "30-second touch" warmup period, we usually did three practice vaults. But in the Olympics, you were allowed only two. Martha and Mary Lee were adjusting the vaulting board and pads and couldn't adjust the equipment as fast as Bela, who had to stay off the floor because he was not an official coach.

But as we hustled to get ready for the vault, we also didn't know which vaults we were supposed to be practicing. Usually Bela or Martha told Dominique Moceanu and me exactly what to do in warmups and in what order. But for some reason, no one knew. I kept looking toward Bela, screaming, "What do we do? Two layouts? An Arabian and a layout? An Arabian and a 1½?"

In the confusion, Dominique and I both did one Arabian and one layout in the warmup. They were pretty easy vaults. But neither of us practiced the vault that we were going to do in the competition—the Yurchenko 1½. When we realized our mistake, it was too late. We hadn't done any vaults the afternoon before or that morning, so we both were getting a little apprehensive.

"Okay, no big deal," I told Dominique. "It will be just like in practice. We've done these vaults a thousand times. I mean, come on. We get two tries. It's going to be fine."

"Yeah, I know," Dominique said. "It'll be fine."

I could tell Dominique was not completely comfortable about skipping the Yurchenko in warmups, especially because she hadn't done a lot of vaulting in the weeks before the Games because of the stress fracture in her leg.

Things just didn't click as they had been earlier. We were not paying too much attention to what the Russians were doing on their last rotation, the floor, but we knew it was one of their best events. The Russians have won so many competitions on the floor over the years, we knew they could easily put up the scores to win it.

Meanwhile, none of our early vaults were quite what we were capable of doing. Shannon's (a 9.7) wasn't her best. Jaycie's (a 9.662) wasn't great. The gold medal was slipping away.

Finally it came down to Dominique Moceanu and me. Dominique stepped up to the top of the vault runway and saluted the judges. I was at the bottom of the stairs, adjusting my wrist supports, stretching and doing a few cartwheels to stay warm. I never saw Dominique's first vault, but I heard a huge collective gasp from the crowd. When I looked up, it seemed all the air had been sucked out of the Georgia Dome.

I looked toward Bela and his face was flushed. Dominique had fallen on her first vault. "Forget it, forget it," Bela was telling Dominique. She nodded her head, but looked shocked.

I looked at Martha and she was wiping her forehead with her hand, shocked and nervous. Everything was hushed as Dominique lined up for her second vault. She began barreling down the runway. Her eyes were so focused, her ponytail bouncing behind her head and her little legs plugging up and down.

And I could not believe what I saw. She fell again, and her score was a 9.2. The gold medal was slipping away.

The Russians were hitting their floor routines and we were struggling. I saw the Russian coaches scurrying about, no doubt asking each other what was going on with the Americans. As I walked up the stairs as the final competitor on the vault, the dome was so quiet that the only noise I could hear was the tapping on the keyboards from all the writers sitting alongside the floor.

For some reason, however, I honestly was not nervous. Not at all. I just thought, "Okay, just do your job. Hit this. Hit this vault." I was confident. I was very deliberate and exacting. I asked Martha to put in the sting mat, a thicker pad, on the landing area. I figured Dominique might have slipped on the regular landing mat, and I didn't want to lose the gold just because of a slippery mat.

I did my regular pre-vault routine. I took a deep breath, visualized the vault, swung my arms in front of me, and lined up exactly 77.3 feet away from my takeoff point.

I started my run and it felt perfect. I hit my second mark—45.8 feet from takeoff—in full stride, perfectly. The vault felt good, too. I went into my round-off, flipped into the vaulting board, pushed off, twisted, and stayed tight.

But then I felt myself pulling my arms open a little too soon. I thought I was higher than I really was. The floor came up on me so quickly, I had no chance of landing the vault cleanly.

When I hit the floor and fell backwards, I heard something rip inside my left ankle. I was humiliated at first, not believing that I had choked that vault. I hadn't fallen on a competition vault in more than a year. I had been automatic on the Yurchenko for months, never missing it once. In Olympic and World Championship competitions, I hadn't fallen, period. Ever.

But there I was, that spotlight that I finally wanted shining on me, looking for a place to hide under the mats. Then there was the pain. It was a really weird pain. Certainly I've had all sorts of pains in my life, but this pain was like none I had ever had before.

My foot felt out of place, as if it had been separated from the rest of my leg. I thought I was going to go crazy for a few seconds; then I shook my foot out and everything was fine again.

But when I picked myself off the mat and saluted the judges, I realized that something was really wrong.

I knew the entire nation wanted to see me hit my second vault. I knew we needed that second vault. I knew how long I had waited to be in the position I was in. But my foot just wasn't right.

As I walked back to the top of the runway, I told Martha, "My foot, my foot."

She thought I was just embarrassed because of the fall. She said, "You're okay, Kerri. Shake it out."

"No, you don't understand!" I said. I looked toward Bela and he knew I really was not okay.

"Okay, Kerri, can you shake it?" he said. "Shake it out, Kerri. You can do it. One more. You can do it, Kerri. Can you shake it out?"

The crowd was stunned silent. I thought for a moment, "What are my parents thinking? Mom must be going crazy." By the time I managed to get back to the start of the runway, my leg was numb. The Russians were still hitting everything. I turned my back to Bela and Martha and said a prayer.

"Please, God, help me out here," I said. "I'm just asking you once here. I've always tried to be a good person. I've always tried to do what's right. Please, just let me do this vault."

I went through my regular routine again. I looked toward Bela, took a deep breath, visualized the vault, swung my arms in front of me, and lined up exactly 77.3 feet away from my takeoff point. I reached down and twisted my left foot with my hand, trying to work out the pain, but all I felt was a crackling.

The green light came on and I thought to myself, "You can and you will do this."

I began my run and honestly could not feel my leg. I was afraid I was going to fall right there on the runway in front of a billion people. It felt like my ankle was swinging loosely from the rest of my leg, like it was hanging by a string. It felt as if I was running so slow, but when I got to my mark at 45.8 feet, I hit it perfectly.

I kept running and hit my mark in front of the vaulting board. I went into the Yurchenko and it seemed I was doing every move at half speed. I just did it by feel, I guess. I didn't feel like I had any power or height. I managed to stay tight and twist strong. And this time when I pulled my legs under me for the landing, I had more room to stick my feet into the mat.

I slammed into the floor a little short, but clean, and immediately I heard another big rip in my ankle.

I thought for sure my leg had snapped in two. Instinctively, maybe because I had done it thousands of times since the first time Lisa showed me how when I was three years old, I hopped into the finishing pose. I did it standing on just my right foot, like a flamingo. But I threw my shoulders back, stuck out my chin, stretched out my arms, and saluted the judges. Tears were already filling my eyes and the heat inside my leg was incredible. I saw one judge cover her face with her hands. The pain knocked me to the mat, a pulsating, pull-your-hair-out, you're-going-to-die pain. I knew for sure I was going to at least faint. There was such a hot rush up my leg. You know how sometimes a pain is so intense, you feel you're on the verge of going crazy? That's how I felt. I started crawling as fast as I could toward the stairs, looking for Bela. I finally found him standing on the other side of the barrier that circled the floor and I just nodded my head at him.

Then Martha and Barb Pearson, a team trainer, reached me and I screamed at them to take off my shoe and cut the tape from my ankle. Then I said, "Is it legal? Are they going to count it as a fall? Are they going to count the vault as a fall?"

A bunch of volunteers surrounded me and put me on a stretcher. I just kept screaming, "Take this shoe off, take this shoe off." As I looked up, all I could see was the bright lights at the top of the Georgia Dome. People moved in front of me to ask all sorts of questions. Photographers flashed more lights in my face.

They took me into a training room underneath the stands, and Mom and Dad got there. I kept asking, "What's wrong? What's wrong? Did they count it as a fall?"

Then Bela and Kathy Kelly arrived and started screaming at me, "We won! We won!" Bela told me, "Kerri, you did it! You did it!"

I scored a 9.712. The vault and the unbelievably wild reaction from the crowd were more than the Russian team could overcome. Had I not been able to do my second vault, the Russians could have won the gold with a couple of 9.9s. But after I hit it, the best their final two performers could come up with was a 9.725 and a 9.5.

That was the happiest moment of my life. And it was the most pain I ever felt. Bela kept telling the trainers, "Do something. Can you do something?"

Someone came in and told Bela and Kathy that they were getting ready to begin the medal ceremony. I looked at Bela and told him, "No! They can't start, I have to go. They can't have it now! I have to go. We just won the gold." Someone told Bela and Kathy that the ceremony had to happen right then, and if I couldn't make it, they'd do something later to present me my medal.

I started crying even more from both the pain and the disappointment, but then Kathy told everyone in the room, "Look, this kid just won the medal for us. She's going out there."

Bela told me, "Kerri, you're going out there. You just put those gold medals in your country's hands. Even if I have to carry you, you're going out there."

Sure enough, that's what he did. During the chaos, trainers put a plastic immobilizing cast on my leg. Someone put a USA warmup jacket on me. Bela swooped me up and carried me to the staging area.

Meanwhile, I started thinking crazy thoughts, probably because of the pain I was in. I told Bela that I didn't want to be different from the rest of the girls. I kept asking for my warmup pants and official shoes. I told Bela to put me down so I could march in with the rest of the team. When we reached the other girls, I reminded them to be sure and line up in the right order, shortest to tallest.

But then the music began playing and the curtain opened, six girls marching in front and Bela carrying me.

"Smile, be happy, Kerri, you just won a gold medal," Bela told me. The crowd stood and applauded. The spotlight was shining on our faces. When I heard the "USA, USA" chant, I smiled broadly.

I looked at Bela and leaned forward to give him a kiss on the cheek. I just kept waving. The whole time, the pain was intense. The noise and emotion coming from the crowd was the best I ever experienced, but I had no idea anyone was clapping at anything I did individually. I had no clue I had had any big impact at all. I kept thinking, "We did it."

When they gave us the medals and played the national anthem, I got very emotional. I told myself, "You've been waiting for this all your life. Thank you, God." At that point, I don't remember feeling any pain in my leg.

We huddled together on the awards stand after the anthem and Shannon said, "We did it, you guys. This is awesome." Shannon and Dominique Moceanu helped me down from the medal platform and Bela carried me around the dome one more time.

The lights kept flashing in my face the whole time we marched off the floor. Even though this was a terrific moment, before we got off the floor, I whispered into Bela's ear, "What about all-arounds? I need some ice. I *have* to do all-arounds."

I had finally qualified for individual all-arounds, but it looked as if my ankle injury would shatter that hope. I could not accept it. In my mind, I thought ice would take care of everything. When we got off the floor, I was put in an ambulance and taken to Crawford Long Hospital. Mom and Dad went with me and I still was asking for ice.

When we got to the hospital, I was given pain-killers and underwent a few X-rays. As I sat in an examining room waiting to hear the results of the tests, I became frantic about finally making the all-arounds, but injuring my ankle. "This is the Olympics. What if it's broken?" I asked Dad. "What about all-arounds and event finals?"

"As far as I'm concerned," my father said, "you have already helped your team win seven gold medals. You helped put those medals around your teammates' necks. Don't worry about all-arounds."

It seemed like forever to get the results of the X-rays, but finally the doctors came back and said my ankle was not broken. "Yes!" I shouted. "I can do it. Let's go see the trainer. I need some ice."

But Dad said the doctors had told him I had done serious damage to my ankle, probably torn some ligaments and tendons, and would be out for a long time. A USOC publicist said a bunch of reporters were in the lobby of the hospital and more were at the interview tent back at the Georgia Dome, waiting for me. I wondered why anyone would go to such lengths to talk to me. Wasn't what they got from the six other girls enough? I had no idea the world was already making such a big deal about my vault. I just did my job.

Somebody else mentioned that my teammates were celebrating the gold medal at Planet Hollywood downtown, and I certainly wasn't going to miss that. We decided to stop by the media tent on the way to Planet Hollywood.

I was fitted with an immobilizing boot filled with ice. I rode in a wheelchair, my foot elevated. I thought to myself, "Okay, I'll sleep with this boot thing on, tape my ankle real tight, take painkillers, and be fine in the morning."

The questions the media asked seemed strange to me. They kept saying, "Kerri, you won the gold for the U.S." "Kerri, did you ever think you'd become an American hero?" "Kerri, now that you're the new Mary Lou . . . "

I thought, "What? The new Mary Lou?" Hey, I just wanted to get to Planet Hollywood and eat a veggie burger.

When I finally got there, I couldn't believe it. Kevin, his girlfriend Karen, and Lisa were there. So were Sunshine, Ann and Don, and Linda and Rudy Ferlan. Lots of other close friends and family members were everywhere. I couldn't believe it when Bruce Willis and Demi Moore started chanting, "Kerri, Kerri, Kerri," when I was wheeled into the restaurant. I couldn't believe Bruce Willis and Demi Moore even knew my name!

The only bad part about that party was I got to stay for just five minutes. I was just getting ready to order my veggie burger when I heard Martha tell everyone, "Okay, we gotta go. The team leaves together."

I was a little upset, but only briefly, because I figured the quicker we got back to the house, the quicker my rehab could begin. I asked Larry Nassar if he could come to my room that night and start whatever therapy I needed.

It was after 1:00 A.M. already, but he agreed. He and other trainers set up a Tens Unit, a muscle therapy machine, in my room. They hooked up an ice machine and arranged the pillows on my bed so that I could elevate my leg.

When they left, I grabbed my diary. "Today is a day I'll never ever forget," I wrote. "I've been on an emotional roller coaster. The team won an Olympic gold medal. Yes! I'm now an Olympic champion. I still can't believe we actually won.

"It would have been the perfect day for me, but it didn't turn out to be too perfect. On the vault, our last event, we were in the lead, with Dominique Moceanu and me left to vault. Well, somehow she fell on both her vaults. I'm not sure exactly what happened on my first vault, but I sat down, too. I heard a loud pop and crackle in my ankle. I quickly said a prayer to God and the next thing I knew the green light was on. Somehow I was running down the vault runway. I made my vault, but the impact of the landing was too much. I blew out my ankle. I'm kind of bummed, because the pictures are going to look retarded, with me on the awards stand with no pants, a brace, and red eyes. It was still so cool. Being number one in the world is awesome.

"I made all-around finals, but it doesn't look too good right now. I'm praying and hoping a miracle happens. I may not be able to perform. I just can't believe it. Why? I've sacrificed so much. I give it my all in workouts. Why did this have to happen? I wanted this so badly. All my life, I've wanted this. I've worked so hard. Well, it's 2:30 A.M. and we have to get up at five for a TV show. What a day."

I never got to sleep that night. I lay there looking at the ceiling, thinking about everything that had happened and wishing my ankle would get better overnight. I fidgeted with the ice pack on my ankle occasionally, hoping and praying the pain would go away. I looked at the therapy machines in my room, the USA warmup jacket hanging over a chair, the teddy bear I'd brought with me from home, staring back at me from the bed next to me. I thought about the first time I had had this Olympic dream and Lisa helping me flip and fly around the house. I thought about Houston, Orlando, Oklahoma City, Colorado Springs, Montreux, Stuttgart, Paris, Sabae, Barcelona. I thought about all the unbelievable ups and downs and twists and turns that I had experienced along the way. I thought about how happy I was to finally achieve my greatest dream, but how much I wanted to march into the Georgia Dome two days later and reach for another one. I wanted to reach my goal of competing in the individual all-around competition.

13

"You very honestly made me believe that I can accomplish anything, if that's what is in my heart"

❀

When daylight began sneaking through my bedroom window the morning after my vault, I was still lying in bed wide awake. I spent the night lying there hoping my swollen ankle would miraculously improve and feeling proud of what our team had accomplished for the USA. The thrill of winning the gold medal never subsided. The pain in my ankle never subsided, either.

Ever since that strange, sad, wonderful morning, I have come to understand that every day is something to cherish. We should appreciate every day for what it is and never take anything for granted.

Before making the vault and realizing the effects it had on so many people, I had based my entire life on training and planning for the future. There was always something out there on the distant horizon: another workout, another meet, the World Championships, the Olympic Games, individual all-arounds. I loved the thrill of competing and the excitement of gymnastics on a day-to-day basis. But in my mind there was always something in the distance luring me into pushing forward.

How strange, sad, and wonderful it was to realize that no one ever knows where the road leads. How eye-opening it was when I began to be aware that I should enjoy and appreciate the journey as much as the destination.

As I got out of bed and began hobbling around the room to begin the day, the impact my vault had on millions of people became clear. I was getting dressed to appear on the *Today* show, which was coming to our house for interviews, when someone brought me the Atlanta newspaper. There were so many nice stories and kind words about me on almost every page. I read a few other newspapers and watched television for the first time since landing the vault. I could not believe the reaction from Americans and others around the world. The night before, I had not gotten a true sense of the impact of my vault, as I was being rushed from the dome to the hospital to the interview tent and then to Planet Hollywood. But almost everything I saw on television the next morning showed my vault or Bela carrying me to the awards platform or fans and coaches talking about how touched they were by the moment. Honestly, I was the one who was touched very deeply, and I still am every day of my life.

Bela said he was stunned by how much courage I showed. Geza said they should stop the Olympics after my "act of heroism," because no other athlete in the Games would show the courage I did. Reggie Miller, the Dream Team superstar, complimented me and said, "I have to meet that Kerri Strug."

There were so many kind things said, I cannot remember them all. True, it was a head-spinning experience, but it was one that made me proud because I believed that I was having a positive effect on all the little girls out there bouncing around their own homes, just like I once did. I was being called the image of the Olympic Games. I was being called the next Mary Lou and Nadia. It was very humbling.

And it all felt strange in a way, because as I was getting the attention and already hearing about talk shows, agents, fans, and movie producers trying to contact me or my parents, I really didn't believe I did anything particularly special. In my mind, I just competed. I tried to help the team win a medal and then to make individual all-arounds. I just tried to hit my routine. That's all I ever wanted. I also thought it was ironic that everything was happening because of an injury I sustained. I thought, "Hey, I've been hurt a lot. This only adds one more to the long list."

I wasn't trying to become the next Mary Lou or Nadia. I merely put out the fire that had been burning in my heart for a lifetime. I reached my ultimate goal.

It also was a very sad time for me as I limped out of my room and went downstairs to the *Today* show set. The last thing I ever wanted was for that vault to be the end of my Olympic Games. If anything, I wanted it to be more of a beginning— vaulting me, so to speak, to a three- or four-medal performance. I easily qualified for individual all-arounds when I hit the vault, finally making up for the bitter disappointment in Barcelona. I also qualified for floor and vault finals. But here I was, hardly able to walk. I was both happy for the moment, but tortured by the fact that I was probably going to miss all-around finals and quite possibly the vault and floor finals, too. As much as I had closed the emotional wounds left open in Barcelona, I didn't want to leave Atlanta without achieving all my goals.

The initial diagnosis on my ankle was a third-degree lateral sprain, but I knew it was much more than a sprain. The entire inside portion of my left foot and leg was already turning black and blue, from the arch of my foot to halfway up my shin.

Only later when I had more comprehensive tests did I learn that there was extensive ligament and tendon damage. As we went to the NBC set for the show, all I knew was that I was going to keep my leg iced and elevated as much as I could and somehow try to make it better. I wanted so desperately to compete, if not in all-arounds, then at least in the vault or floor finals.

As we talked about winning the gold medal during the *Today* interview, I kept my foot elevated. Afterward, I changed the ice and went for more interviews at an Olympic hospitality room sponsored by a Karolyi team supporter from Houston, Jim McIngvale. I sat in a recliner with my leg elevated, doing several radio talk shows. Mr. McIngvale and others picked me up and carried me in the recliner from interview to interview. I'm sure I looked funny sitting there in a La-Z-Boy, being lifted and carried from table to table, like Cleopatra.

When I got back to the house at Emory, I begged trainers to do whatever they could to get my ankle well enough to compete.

"Try anything," I told Larry Nassar.

I knew that competing in the all-arounds was unrealistic because it was just one day away. But when coaches and trainers asked how I felt, I held out hope. I told them that I thought my ankle would improve in time for the competition. I spent thirty minutes out of every hour icing my leg. The rest of the time I spent lying down, elevating it or undergoing electronic stimulation and ultrasound on the ankle. I occasionally stood up and tried to flex my foot, standing on my tiptoes and working it out.

I was emotionally torn between the high of hitting the vault and the frustration of injuring my ankle. When my teammates went to an afternoon workout, I stayed in my room, either with ice or a therapy machine on my ankle the entire time. The press continued to call, wanting to talk about the vault and the team gold. I loved to accommodate them, but the most important thing on my mind was getting well.

I spoke with Mom on the telephone and she said there were dozens upon dozens of messages and faxes at their hotel from agents, publicity people, and marketers from all over the country. They were receiving interview requests from every imaginable media outlet. When she first told me about all the attention, I really didn't understand how overwhelming it had become. I was isolated in the house and was more concerned about the competition.

I spent most of the time talking to my mom about my disappointment over all-arounds, and she said she would come see me the next day. After we hung up, I was doing a telephone interview with Susan Rook for the CNN show *Talk Back Live* when Bela came storming into my room holding a cellular phone.

"Kerri, hang up the phone! Hang up the phone!" he said.

"What? I can't hang up the phone, I'm on live TV," I told him.

"You have to hang up the phone, the president is on the line. He wants to talk to you."

Talk Back Live was on a commercial break, so I asked a producer who also was on the phone, "What should I do? The president is waiting to talk to me." He told me to talk with the president and then call back later.

I nervously picked up the cell phone and said, "Hello?"

"Kerri, this is President Clinton. How's your ankle?"

"It hurts, but I'm sure it will be okay."

The president went on to tell me that he had watched me compete and was proud of the way I showed courage. He said I exhibited a true American spirit and that he and the entire nation were proud of me.

All I could do was keep saying, "Thank you, thank you," until finally I got up enough nerve to mention to the president, "I know the Olympic team is coming to the White House after the Games. Can I get a picture with you?"

He said that he would be coming to Atlanta to watch the individual all-arounds the next day and he would be happy to meet our entire team. I was thrilled.

The next morning my ankle had not improved much, if at all. I went to work out with my teammates, realizing that I could hardly walk, let alone do all-arounds that evening. But I was still hoping to make the vault and floor finals. I stretched and went through therapy. I tried a few simple moves, a few walkovers, but the pain was still severe.

"It's not going to happen," Bela told me.

"I know," I said.

I went back to the house and my mom came to see me. We sat on the edge of my bed talking and I began to cry as she held me.

"I haven't achieved all my goals: a team gold *and* the individual all-arounds," I told her.

"Kerri, in life sometimes you don't reach all your goals," she said. "You have to be thankful that you have already accomplished something unforgettable."

I still wanted so badly to make it back into the competition, but I understood what she meant. I reached one very important goal that affected millions, maybe billions, of people. I never could have planned for something like my vault to happen, but it did. I had to accept it and appreciate what it meant to people and to me.

I was already getting piles of letters and gifts in the mail. People were sending me teddy bears and flowers. Someone sent me a pair of crutches. The letters were so touching and considerate. I read as many as I could as I was treating my ankle. I also was doing interview after interview.

I did go to individual all-arounds that night, but I sat in a skybox, with my foot resting on a pillow on a table with a therapy machine. Dominique Moceanu took my place in the lineup and I had tears in my eyes throughout the entire first portion of the competition. Shannon finished eighth overall, Dominique Moceanu ninth, and Dominique Dawes seventeenth. After the competition, our entire team met privately with the president, which gave us all a thrill. I did get a picture with him and he was very kind and complimentary to all of us.

I went back to the room still feeling somewhat down, but then something else happened—something very sad that again helped me learn to appreciate every day for what it was. It also put my ankle injury in perspective.

My mom, my dad, Kevin, and Kevin's girlfriend, Karen Pendlebury, were walking through Olympic Centennial Park after the all-around competition. Kevin and Karen stopped to listen to some music and mentioned to my parents that they wanted to stay and watch the entire concert. Mom said she was tired and would rather go back to the hotel, so they all left. About an hour later, a bomb went off in the park, killing two people, injuring others, and sending shivers up everyone's spine.

My ankle injury did not seem quite so significant anymore. I watched news of the bombing in horror, like everyone else. And the next day, it was easier to come to grips with reality.

My parents said the telephone was still ringing constantly, to the point that if they left the room for just a couple of hours, there would be fifty more messages when they returned.

"Kerri, what do you think you want to do?" Mom asked me on the telephone. "Everyone is telling us some amazing things about what this could mean for you. They're saying this is a once-in-a-lifetime opportunity. We're getting overwhelmed and confused."

I *hate* being unprepared. But nothing could have prepared me for the opportunities that were suddenly coming my way. People were telling my parents some staggering things. It was strange, because I had spent my entire life meticulously planning things out in my mind. But now I had to consider changing those plans almost overnight. And it wasn't solely because of the commercial opportunities that I became intrigued by the offers. As everyone in the sport already knew, money alone never swayed me from wanting to fulfill my dream of competing at UCLA. Yes, after my vault the money people were mentioning was much more significant than anything I had ever been offered before. If what they were saying was true, it was going to be enough to pay for college and establish a foundation for the rest of my life. But the idea that I could affect the sport in a positive way also had me thinking about the possibilities. I never forgot the influence Nadia and Mary Lou had had on me when I was beginning the journey that led to Atlanta.

Nadia's movie was inspiring. Mary Lou's story and the way she used her position to become an exceptional motivational speaker helped athletes and gymnastics immeasurably. Suddenly I was in a position to truly make a difference not just for gymnasts, but for athletes and people in all walks of life. The mountains of letters I was receiving every day from all over the world helped convince me of the magnitude of my vault. I was hearing from little girls and boys, teenagers, parents, grandparents, clergymen, even prison inmates. I was getting cards and letters from Japan, England, Australia, India, Canada, Germany, and every corner of the world.

Most everyone who wrote said I inspired them with my vault. It was marvelous reading those letters and understanding that I could make a difference in people's lives. "It is inexplicable to me why I felt the need to write you," one letter said. "But I did. You very honestly made me believe that I can accomplish anything, if that's what is in my heart."

That letter was from a ninety-year-old man from Idaho. I thought to myself, "Here's a man in his nineties feeling inspired to keep dreaming because of something I did."

I had no choice but to think about the opportunities before me. My mom said she would begin asking for help from friends in gymnastics and the media about what we should do and which agents and offers seemed most sincere.

At the same time, as a team we were beginning to get some remarkable offers. Since Amy and I were the only amateurs on the team, she and I began feeling pressured to turn professional in order for the team to take advantage of its moment. There was talk about featuring our team on the cover of a Wheaties cereal box. The post-Olympic gymnastics tour also was rumored to be expanding from twenty-nine cities to sixty because of our gold medal. Someone from *The Tonight Show* contacted my mom and me and asked if I would appear on the show. We scheduled a date to appear on the show and then they asked if I would promise that Jay Leno's show would be the first late-night show I did.

"Sure," I said.

There were all sorts of other offers for each of us. Pressure kept building for Amy and me to give up our amateur status and help the entire team capitalize on our win. Amy asked me, "What are you going to do? Should we do this together?"

I had no idea. One thing I knew for sure was that I did not want to put off going to UCLA for another year or even for another semester; since I had already taken the past year off to train for the Olympics. That was nonnegotiable. Whatever happened would have to be worked around my class schedule.

I also knew that I wanted to take my time making the decision, especially since vault finals were one day away, floor finals were a day after that, and my ankle was still not improving fast enough.

Somehow finding a way to get my ankle better was my highest priority. The team went for more photos and interviews on July 27, including a shoot with *Time* magazine. Even as we were on the floor posing for the pictures, I kept my ankle elevated. At workouts, I did mostly conditioning and a little bars, but spent most of my time lying on my back, with my ankle hooked up to one machine or another. I got back to the house and walked up and down the stairs, trying to work it out. As part of my treatment I went to the Emory University swimming pool, hoping to flex my ankle and walk in the water to stimulate my recovery. The USA synchronized swimming team was finishing their workouts, and they really lifted my spirits. Actually, they lifted me. Someone asked, "Hey, can we do a few lifts with you?" They picked me up out of the water as if I was part of the routine, and it was a lot of fun. But when I got back to the house, I realized that what I did with the synchro team was about as difficult as my ankle could stand. It was not improving as rapidly as I had hoped.

The next day, I couldn't compete in the vault finals. A day later, my ankle was still not well enough for the floor exercise finals, either. I withdrew an hour before the competition, but at least I got to walk to the center of the floor and address the crowd, which received me with great warmth. "Unfortunately, because of my ankle, I won't be able to compete," I said. "But I wanted to thank you all for all the support you have shown the last few days."

I had qualified for floor finals with the highest combined floor score in the competition. I truly believed that I could have won the gold medal on floor, but it was not meant to be. I told Mom and Dad later, "All those days practicing on that hard floor at the ranch. All that work. All I had to do was one more routine and I could have won a medal." I was really devastated.

With my competition now definitely over, we turned to the many other questions left to answer. My teammates continued to ask if I had made a decision about my amateur status. I was hearing that we won the medal as a team, so we should move on to other opportunities as a team. In the meantime, my parents were trying to sort through all the agents that were contacting them. They got advice from friends we knew in the business and pared the hundreds of contacts down to just a few names. We spoke with several agents and then made the decision to renounce my amateur status. We chose Leigh Steinberg, because he was straightforward and answered all our questions. We made it clear we did not want to compromise integrity for money. He told us about all the charitable organizations with which his clients have become involved. It also helped that Leigh was based in the Los Angeles area, not too far from UCLA.

The remainder of my stay in Atlanta was a whirlwind of activity, with interviews and appearances every day and the letters and gifts arriving nonstop. But four memories stand out more than the rest and will stay with me forever. And this time, I have the pictures to prove it.

I had a chance to formally say good-bye to all the fans who cheered for us at the Olympic Gymnastics Gala exhibition on July 30. I waved to the crowd and did a few handstands, walkovers, and dance elements with my teammates while wearing an air cast. We danced to "Georgia on My Mind" and were presented with flowers by the Russian men's team. I was deeply moved by the reception I received from the crowd.

The next unforgettable memory came after I spoke with a

sportswriter friend and told him about how I had ruined my chance to get some pictures with the Dream Team in Barcelona four years earlier. He knew I was a big basketball fan and he was also friends with some people in the NBA offices. The next thing I knew, our entire team was invited to meet the Dream Team. We went to a downtown hotel where the Dream Team was staying and met with them for almost an hour. I brought a basketball with me—and a camera that I knew how to work, of course—and had them all sign autographs and pose for pictures. It was wonderful. Reggie Miller shook my hand and told me how impressed he was with my vault. Shaquille O'Neal swept me up and lifted me like Bela did on the way to the awards stand. They were all so gracious.

Two days later, I was overwhelmed when I won the Olympic Spirit Award along with track legend Carl Lewis. Every four years the award is given to a male and a female athlete who epitomize the true spirit of the Games.

And finally, perhaps my most lasting memory came when I got to go to the closing ceremonies of the Olympic Games. It was a little awkward, because my six teammates did not want to go. They had to take an early flight to New York in order to appear on *The David Letterman Show*, so they stayed at the house. I wished I could go with them to New York, but I had already promised *The Tonight Show* that I would appear there first, and I did not want to go back on my word. The silver lining about missing the trip with my teammates was that I was finally able to attend an Olympic ceremony. Regretfully, I had missed both the opening and closing ceremonies in Barcelona and the opening ceremonies in Atlanta.

I finally was getting a taste of the flavor of the Games. I went to Centennial Olympic Stadium with Kathy Kelly and had an absolutely terrific time. The USA softball players and swimmers adopted me into their groups and we sat there marveling at the show and celebrating our experiences. It was a spectacular show, with music, fireworks, extravagant production numbers, and the athletes at the center of it all, dancing and enjoying our night together.

It made up for all the parties I ever had to miss because of training. It made up for those holidays away from home. It even made up for my eighth birthday party, when all I wanted was to watch the *Nadia* video, but became so frustrated when my friends left me. It was a night that sent me on my way to the real world and all the strange, sad, and wonderful things we all experience every day.

I regret nothing about my gymnastics career. Each step backward made me want to charge forward that much more. Each experience, good or bad, meant something to me, and I learned from them all. The sacrifices and challenges prepared me for that unforgettable evening in Atlanta. Isn't it funny how one split second, one incredible moment, changes everything? Even now I am not sure I would have chosen the fate that blindsided me in Atlanta, but not many people can pinpoint a single moment in time at which their entire life jumped one track and began charging down another. And very few people have had that moment replayed to the world a million times on video. Atlanta changed everything for me.

When I got to Tucson after the Games, my hometown treated me to a remarkable Kerri Strug Day. There was a parade in my honor, with thousands of fans lining the street, bands, and speeches; everyone showed me a lot of love. When I got home, I received a letter from former President Reagan, and in it he said, "Your determination, perseverance, and unyielding sense of commitment to your team helped lead the United States to victory. You should be proud of yourself, not simply because your team won the gold, but because you went to Atlanta with a goal and you endured to the end."

Everything I had to endure was worth it. The challenges did not end in Atlanta, but the years leading up to my Olympic experience helped me understand and deal with every challenge I would face in life.

After the Games, there were setbacks and misunderstandings that I wished hadn't happened. I became somewhat estranged from my teammates for a while, because I joined a rival gymnastics tour from the one in which they participated. I joined the other tour because it allowed me to go to school during the week and perform on weekends. The tour in which my teammates participated had weekday performances, and my teammates had to postpone college plans in order to participate. That's something I never wanted to do.

The media said that I was being placed above my teammates. In every interview I ever have done since the Games, I mention that we won the gold medal as a team. When I won the ESPY award for the most clutch performance of 1996, I accepted the award and then said, "First, I want to thank my teammates, because I could not have done this without them."

But even when emotions were a bit strained, I believed that the bond we had in Atlanta as teammates would never change. What we did in those Games was historic. For a brief while, that bond was tested. When we were in Washington, D.C., to meet the president after the Games, I went to a studio to pose for a cover photo for *People* magazine.

When I returned to my hotel room, all six of my teammates were there waiting for me. Someone said, "Kerri, we need to talk." They went on to express their frustration over the team being forgotten in all the hoopla over my vault. I promised them that I would continue to mention in every interview that this was a *team* gold. And certainly I did not want to lose any of them as friends.

Eventually, we cleared the air. I think of the whole ordeal like this: We were such a close team in Atlanta, just like sisters. But even sisters sometimes have to work things out. Now we are close again and I am rejoining my Olympic teammates on a gymnastics tour, which this time allows me to perform without affecting my class schedule at UCLA. As always, I am so proud to be part of the magnificent, historic 1996 U.S. gymnastics team. I marvel at Shannon's elegance on bars and beam. I am amazed by Dominique Moceanu's unique talent. Amy's perfection on vault and bars, Jaycie's overall skill, Dominique Dawes's power, and Amanda's personality on beam all make me proud to have shared the Olympic experience with them.

We shared a truly unique moment. I learned to appreciate not just that one day when we won the gold medal, but every day I live. Whether it turns out strange, sad, or wonderful, I wake up to the light sneaking into my room every day and realize that I am one very lucky young lady.

I have been able to meet terrific people: movie stars, athletes, and new friends. I have been able to experience the highs: television shows, personal appearances, and remarkable events. I have seen the bizarre: strange letters and requests, including wedding invitations from strangers and countless people asking if they can carry me like Bela.

I have known the satisfaction of helping people who deserve to be helped, participating in the Disney Dreamers and Doers program, which acknowledges high achievers across the country. I have been able to be a part of the Special Olympics, the Children's Miracle Network, the March of Dimes, the Hugh O'Brian Foundation, the Inner City Games, and other charities.

One of my new best friends is Libby Blamey, a sorority sister (Kappa Alpha Theta) at UCLA who has helped me adapt to the regular life I lead as a college student during the week. Another new friend is a girl named Andrea, who is critically ill and a pen pal. I met Andrea through my association with the Children's Miracle Network, and she awed me with her courage. I promised her that I would give her gymnastics lessons if she went through physical therapy and got well. And I plan to keep that promise. Andrea is one of the many special people I have met on my many weekend appearances. I have been able to have an effect on her and many other people's lives because of what happened in Atlanta.

But as much as the 1996 Olympic Games may have focused the world's attention on me, it has also helped open my eyes to the world. One weekend in December when I was in New York making an appearance on *Saturday Night Live*, my mom called and said I needed to fly to Houston for the holidays instead of going home to Tucson. My father, who had been experiencing fatigue a few days earlier, was having an angioplasty procedure performed. Thank goodness, he came through the procedure like a champion. However, the ordeal shocked me because my dad is the one who seems invincible. He does everything for us and keeps the family together. It opened all our eyes.

A few months later, I was at an event in Utah when my mother called and told me that Hilary Grivich had been killed in an automobile accident. My friend from Bela's, someone who had dreams just like me, was suddenly gone. Sometimes a gold medal doesn't seem very important at all.

When I was competing, I always worried too much about the

things that were coming up in my life. Only moments after accomplishing my goal in Atlanta when I hit my vault, I was worrying and wondering if I could compete in my next events. In the big picture, those things mean little.

Sure, I still look ahead and make plans. But now there is more than one goal in my life, and the plans are flexible. I'm going to live every day to its fullest. I'm trying to do the best I can to keep my balance on a very narrow beam. I'm trying to balance school, friends, family, gymnastics, and sudden notoriety. I'm hoping to get my degree, enter the communications field, and maybe continue to pursue the television and broadcast opportunities that have come my way. I have been fortunate to make appearances on *Beverly Hills* 90210, *Touched by an Angel*, and other shows and have loved the experiences. I'm going to continue to be a good friend to Sunshine, Katie, and Libby. I'm going to try and find a boyfriend (yes, I'm still looking), spend time with my family, and continue to have a positive influence on and really make a difference in people's lives.

God willing, I will probably even travel to Sydney, Australia, for the 2000 Games. Like I've said before, Australia is a country I have always wanted to see. Will I be there as an athlete? I'll have to figure that part out. I think I'll make a list.